F. C. PAVILO

THE COLOUR OF ROME

THE VATICAN • THE SISTINE CHAPEL
TIVOLI • VILLA D'ESTE • VILLA ADRIANA

EDITRICE LOZZI

Foto: Archivio Editrice Lozzi.
Foto pagg. 106-109-113-114-115-123: Archivio Musei Vaticani.
Foto pagg. 7-24: Egidio Gambassi.
Foto pag. 74: Fabio Soldaini.

GENERAL INDEX

BRIEF HISTORICAL OUTLINES

Rome is situated 41° 53' 54" N. lat., 12° 59' 53" E. long., on the banks of the Tiber.

According to Varro's calculations, Rome was founded on April 21, 753 B.C.

Rome was first governed by Kings (753-510 B.C.); then as a Republic by Consuls (510-30) and finally by Emperors (30 B.C. to 476 A.D.) During the Middle Ages, the Church established its temporal rule and Rome remained the seat of the Papal Court until September 20, 1870 when the Italian army entered Rome and the Eternal City became the capital of a united Italy.

The Vatican, a small territory of 0,440 kms.^{2} occupied by St. Peter's Basilica, St. Peter's Square and the Vatican palaces, is under the sovreignty of the Pope, and it has been called the «Vatican City State» since 1929.

Rome has a population of over three millions.

The Kings of Rome. According to the legend, the seven Kings of Rome were: Romulus, Numa Pompilius, Tullus Hostilius, Ancus Martius, Tarquinius Priscus, Servius Tullius, and Tarquinius Superbus.

667. Romans and Albans contesting for superiority agreed to choose three champions on each side to decide the question. The three Horatii, Roman knights, overcame the three Curiatii, Alban knights, and unite Alba to Rome.

509. Tarquin the Proud and his family expelled for tyranny and licentiousness: royalty abolished. The Patricians established an aristocratic commonwealth.

The Republic. First period (510-87 B.C.) from the expulsion of Tarquin to the Dictatorship of Sulla. — Second period (87-30 B.C.) from Sulla to Augustus.

496. The Latins and the Tarquins declared war against the Republic and were defeated at Lake Regillus.

477-396. Wars with Veii and the Etruscans. Veii taken by Camillus after ten years' siege.

390. The Gauls, under Brennus, won a remarkable victory over the Romans on the banks of the little River Allia, after which they sacked and plundered Rome. However, they eventually returned to their own land and Rome was gradually rebuilt (343-290).

264-146. The Punic Wars, which culminated in the destruction of Carthage, the leading naval power in the Mediterranean.

146. The conquest of Greece.

88-86. Fighting between Marius and Sulla. 82-89. Sulla's dictatorship. Decline of the Republican institutions.

60-53. The First Triumvirate: Caesar, Pompey and Crassus.

58. Caesar's campaigns in Gaul and Britain.

48. Pompey was defeated at Pharsalus; Caesar was assassinated on March 15, 44, (the Ides of March) during a Senate Meeting.

43. The Second Triumvirate: Octavian, (the future Augustus), Anthony and Lepidus.

42. Battle of Philippi in Macedonia. Death of Brutus and Cassius.

31. Octavian defeated Anthony and Cleopatra at Actium (Greece); remaining the sole ruler of Rome.

The Empire. The Emperor Octavian (63 B.C.-14 A.D.) took the name of «Caesar Augustus». The birth of Jesus Christ.

The reign of Augustus coincided with the golden age of Latin literature: this was the era of writers such as Cicero, Virgil, Horace, Ovid, Livy and Tacitus.

61. St. Paul visited Rome for the first time, entering the city by the ancient Capena gate. During Nero's persecution (64-68) he was martyred at the same time as St. Peter.

64. Rome was burned in a great fire in Nero's reign and the Christians were blamed for the great fire.

70. Jerusalem was rased to the ground by Titus. Vespasian began to build the Colosseum in 72.

98-117. Under Trajan, the Roman Empire reached its maximum expansion.

117-138. During Hadrian's reign, Rome was at the peak of its architectural splendour.

The Empire began to decline between the 2nd and 3rd centuries, as a result of internal crises and because of pressure from barbarian peoples.

272. Aurelius began to build the Aurelian Walls as

protection against the threat of invasion.

284. Diocletian and Maximian: the first division of the Empire.

312. Constantine the Great allowed the Christians freedom of religious practice. In 331 he transferred the capital of the Empire to Byzantium (Constantinople).

361. Julian the Apostate abjured Christianity and re-opened the pagan temples. He was killed in battle in Persia.

395. The Roman Empire was definitively divided between the East (Arcadius) and the West (Honorius).

404. Transfer of the Capital to Ravenna.

410. Rome sacked by the Goths.

475. Romulus Augustulus, the last Emperor.

476. Odoacer's conquest of Rome put an end to the Roman Empire in the West.

The Middle Ages. 493. The Goths established their reign in Italy, defeating Odoacer.

535-553. The Byzantine-Gothic war.

568. The Lombards invaded Italy: Italy was divided among the barbarians and the Eastern Empire (the Byzantines).

729. With the donation of Sutri by the Lombard king Liutprandus, the temporal rule of the popes began.

800. On Christmas day, Leo III crowned Charlemagne Emperor of the Holy Roman Empire.

1073-1085. Pope Gregory VII, a fervent and energetic reformer, began his fight against the Emperor Henry IV (The War of Investitures).

1084. Rome was invaded and sacked by the Normans, led by Robert Guiscard.

1300. Boniface VIII proclaimed the first Jubilee.

1305. Clement V moved the papal seat from Rome to Avignon, where it remained until 1377.

1377. Cola di Rienzo, the last of the Tribunes, founded the Roman Republic. He was assassinated in 1354.

The Renaissance. 1471. The foundation of the Capitoline Museums, the oldest public collection in the world.

1503-1513. Julius II began to pull down the old St. Peters in order to build the present Basilica, under Bramante's supervision.

1513-1521. Leo X, the son of Lorenzo the Magnificent, made Rome the greatest cultural centre. — Under the pontificate of Leo X the Lutheran Reform began. — The imperial invasion of Italy and the disastrous Sack of Rome (16 May, 1527) put an end to the golden age of the papal city in a nightmare of fire and blood.

1585-1590. Sixtus V, a real innovator of town planning, covered Rome with new buildings.

The Modern and Contemporary Age. 1799. The Jacobine Republic in Rome, Pope Pius VI was deported to France.

1800. The First Restoration: Pius VII was reestablished in Rome.

1809. Rome came once more under French hegemony.

1814. The Restoration brought back Pius VII to Roman soil.

1849. The Roman Republic led by the Triumvirate: Mazzini, Armelini, Saffi. Giuseppe Garibaldi was in command of the army.

1849. French troops put an end to the Republican government after seven months, and restored Pius IX to the papal throne.

1861. On March 27, the Italian Parliament declared Rome the natural capital of the new State.

1870. On September 20, Italian troops entered Rome through the breach in Porta Pia.

1929. On February 11, the «Roman Question» between the Church and the State was finally resolved by the Lateran Treaty, which came to be part of the Constitution of the Italian Republic.

1943. The neighbourhood of St. Lawrence, was particularly damaged by bombing during the 2nd World War and there were many victims.

1946. In Italy, the Republic was proclaimed in accordance with the June 2 referendum.

1962-65. The Ecumenical Council, Vatican II, was summoned by John XXIII and concluded by Paul VI.

1978. After the death of Paul VI and the pontificate of John Paul I which lasted one month, John Paul II the Polish Pope, acceded to the pontifical throne. He is the first non-Italian Pope for more than four and a half centuries.

THE CAPITOLINE HILL

THE IMPERIAL FORUMS

THE COLOSSEUM

THE ROMAN FORUM

The Capitol, once sacred to the Romans and the destination of the triumphal processions of victorious generals, is today the headquarters of the Mayor and the Municipality of Rome. In spite of changing events and historic conditions, the * **CAPITOLINE HILL** has remained the basic nucleus of Roman life for thousands of years. It is reached by the grand flight of steps known as the «Cordonata», built to a design by Michelangelo especially for the triumphal entry of the Emperor Charles V in 1536.

The bronze statue of **Cola di Rienzo**, is by Masini. It is placed on fragments of ancient remains, to show that the last Roman Tribune wanted to re-establish the Republic on the ruins of the Empire. The statue was erected in 1887 presumably on the spot where the Tribune was killed by the people. At the top of the stairs are the colossal groups of the **Dioscuri,** Castor and Pollux, found near the Ghetto and placed here in 1583 by Gregory XIII. Sixtus V added the **Trophies of Marius** and the **statues of Constantine** and his son **Constantine Caesar.** We now reach **Piazza del Campidoglio,** designed by Michelangelo for the munificent Pope Paul III (1534-1549). The old artist placed on a new pedestal the equestrian statue of **Marcus Aurelius** (161-180), the only one of the many bronze equestrian statues once adorning Rome that has survived. In his equestrian statue, removed in 1981 for some delicate restoration, the Emperor-Philosopher appears so august, so worthy of governing that none can refuse to pay him homage. It is commonly believed that this statue owes its preservation to the

fact that is was, thought to have been the statue of Constantine, the first Christian Emperor. It came to light in the Lateran, in the house of Verus, a descendent of Marcus Aurelius. Michelangelo had it moved in 1538. It was gilded: and the people believe that when the gilt returns to the horse, the end of the world will be imminent.

This splendid square was conceived by Michelangelo, who also designed the two palaces on the opposite sides of the square, whose divergence creates a widening perspective which is most effective.

The Palazzo Senatorio at the back of the square, was built in the 13th century on the ancient ruins of the Tabularium. Its present facade was designed by Giacomo della Porta and made by Girolamo Rainaldi. Michelangelo designed the flight of steps. The fountain, adorned with three statues, the **Tiber** and the **Nile** on either side and **Rome Triumphant** (of over modest proportions) in the centre, was added in 1588 by Matteo di Castello. The Senators, Palace is the Mayor's residence.

Rising from it is the **Capitoline Tower,** built in 1579 by Martino Longhi, where the famous bell, the «Patarina», once hung.

The two lateral palaces house the **CAPITOLINE MUSEUM** which contains a very rich collection of classical marbles, the oldest public collection in the world (1471).

In the courtyard of the **Palazzo Nuovo,** on the left for those who have·climbed the «Cordonata», we see among other things, the statue of Marforio, one of the «talking» statues of Rome, like the

Aerial view of the Capitol

more famous Pasquino. A broad stairway leads to the first floor.

In the centre of the first room, the **Dying Gaul** lies in agony, a marble copy of the bronze statue of the Hellenistic King Attalus I of Pergamon (3rd century B.C.); the simple, natural position of the body, the features of the face which express deep anguish while they reveal human strength, everything blends marvellously to make this statue one of the most significant examples of Hellenistic sculpture.

The well known group of **Love and Psyche,** an enchanting Hellenistic work, shows the chaste kiss of young lovers, the sculpture is a copy of a 2nd century original. The **Satyr** is the best copy of an original bronze statue by Praxiteles, who had the divine gifts of tender beauty and grace.

Second and third rooms: various sculptured works of art. The fourth, or philosophers' room, contains many busts of Greek and Roman writers and warriors. In the centre, the seated statue is believed to be **M. Claudius Marcellus,** one of the Roman generals of the Second Punic War who, after a long siege, occupied Syracuse, where the famous Greek scientist Archimedes rendered useless the powerful machines of the Romans. Among the many busts, four are of the great epic poet of Greece, **Homer,** who sang the heroes of Troy, and was disputed as citizen by seven cities. Tradition represents him as a poor blind man. **Socrates,** the celebrated Athenian philosopher, is here with his flat nose, thick lips, protruding eyes, like a satyr. Before drinking the fatal poisoned cup, he had already set forth his idea of the immortality of the soul.

The fifth room, or «room of the Emperors», contains about eighty busts of Roman Emperors and Empresses; it is the most interesting portrait gallery in existence. The name of Caesar is commonly given to the first twelve Emperors. These who, when we were in school, seemed like myths to us, now become men of yesterday through their life-like busts in this room. Art has made them our contemporaries.

The «Room of Venus»:

The **Capitoline Venus** was found in the Suburra in the 17th century. It is perhaps the most plea-

sing presentation of all the goddesses; here we admire her in all her beauty, full of charm and grace. It is in the style of Praxiteles.

The «Room of the Doves»:

The **mosaic of the Doves** was found in Hadrian's Villa at Tivoli and was at once recognized as the one described by the naturalist Plinius. It might even be taken for a painting, so fine is the work.

In the lovely figure of a **Maiden clasping a Dove to her Breast,** when attacked by a snake, we see a symbol of the human soul making the choice between good and evil.

The **Palace of the Conservatori** contains innumerable artistic treasure.

The first room was painted by Giuseppe Cesari, Cav. d'Arpino. He worked here for more than forty years. The other rooms were painted by Laurenti, Daniele da Volterra, Caracci, etc. The admirable statue of the **Cavaspina** (Boy extracting a Thorn from his Foot) in the third room, belongs to the pre-Phidian period. It is probably the best surviving statue of that time.

The **Wolf** (fourth room), the symbol of Rome, is an Etruscan work which dates from the 5th century B.C. In the 15th century, during the first flowering of the Renaissance, the Tuscan sculptor, Pollaiolo added the figures of two babies, who represent Romulus and Remus.

The **Pinacoteca Capitolina,** picture gallery, countains some important masterpieces, among others: Romulus and Remus, by Rubens; Cleopatra and Augustus, by Guercino; The Rape of Europa, by Paolo Veronese; St. Sebastian, by Guido Reni; St. Petronilla, by Guercino; Magdalene, by Tintoretto; portraits by Van Dyck, etc.

S. MARIA D'ARACOELI rises on the highest point of the Capitol, site of the Rock or Citadel of Rome. A legend relates that Augustus raised an altar here to the «Son of God», to recall the oracle of the Sibyl about the coming of the Saviour. This church inherited the glory of the ancient Capitol; it became the national church of the nobility and people of Rome, the principal seat of the medieval Senate, whence the laws of Rome were proclaimed.

The bronze EQUESTRIAN STATUE OF MARCUS AURELIUS, the only surviving statue of the many that adorned ancient Rome.

The «Capitoline Basilica» is very picturesque with its secular relics, its tombs, its frescoes, its gilded ceiling and ancient trappings. It originally belonged to the Greek monks, then to the Benedictine Fathers until 1250, when it was given to the Franciscans. It is reached by a staircase of 124 steps that was built in 1348 as an offering to the Blessed Virgin for freeing Rome from the plague. The elaborate sixth-century gold-coffered ceiling was built to celebrate the triumph of Marcantonio Colonna, who in 1571 led the Christian fleet to victory over the Turks in the famous Battle of Lepanto.

On the left of the transept, the octagonal chapel dedicated to **St. Helena** marks the place of the other altar of the Augustan legend. Right under the altar of **St. Helena**, at a level 15 cm. (6 in.) lower than the present pavement, there is a white marble altar, embellished with sculptures and

A characteristic view of VIA DEI FORI IMPERIALI, seen through two of the Colosseum's arches. The ARCH OF TITUS can be seen on the left against the green background of the PALATINE.

The CAPITOLINE SHE-WOLF is the symbol of Rome. Legend has it that Romulus and Remus, the sons of Mars, were saved and nursed by a she-wolf. Romulus founded Rome on the 21st April in 753 B.C.

mosaics. They illustrate scenes of the above-mentioned legend which can be interpreted with the help of the scenes on the table of the altar. It dates from the 12th century.

In a small chapel in the sacristy, the * **Holy Child** is kept. A poetic legend narrates that a Franciscan friar who lived in Jerusalem, one day made a statue of the Child Jesus in olive wood. He was sad for he had no colours with which to paint it, but during the night angels came down and painted it for him. The friar brought the statue back with him, the boat sank off the coast of Leghorn and the precious box was lost. But after a few days, it was miraculously washed upon the beach. Thus the good friar was able to bring it to the Aracoeli Church.

During the Christmas festivities, the Child is placed in the artistic crib prepared in the second chapel of the nave, on the left. Roman children go there to recite the traditional «sermons».

On going out by the main door, we admire the large staircase erected in 1348, the Romanesque façade and a splendid panorama of the city.

PIAZZA VENEZIA, the heart of Rome and the heart of Italy, takes its name from the **Palazzo Venezia** which the Venetian Paul II (1461-1471), a lover of munificence, had built in 1455 while he was still a cardinal. It was the first great Renaissance palace of Rome, and it was enriched by outstanding art works. It was a typical example of this first Renaissance period and it marked the transition to a modern palace from the mediaeval fortified dwelling place, of which it retains certain features. The * **Victor Emmanuel II Monument** also called the «Vittoriano», was

11

designed by Giuseppe Sacconi (1885-1911). It rises at the foot of the Capitol in the heart of Rome, where it was squeezed in, altering the ancient relationship between this hill and the neighbouring district, with its massive dimension. The Venetian sculptor Chiaradia, worked for twenty years on the equestrian statue of the King which was completed, after his death by Gallori (1901). The elaborate bas-reliefs at the base which represent the most illustrious Italian cities, were designed by Maccagnani, who for many years collaborated with Sacconi in carving the three-dimensional ornaments. The building's two colossal **wings** are surmounted by winged victories, whose dark bronze contrasting with the bright marble and clearly visible against the panorama of Rome, were made in 1908 by Carlo Fontana and Paolo Bartolini. In the centre is the **Altar of the Fatherland** crowned by the statue of Rome at whose feet since 1921, lies the **Tomb of the Unknown Soldier.**

To the left of the «Vittoriano» is a **fragment of a tomb** in travertine marble, which was erected to Caius Publicius Bibulos «for his honour and courage» as the inscription state (1st century B.C.). From the square begins the **Via dei Fori Imperiali,** a broad, straight stretch built in 1932, cutting through the ruins of the forums from which it takes its name. A proposal has recently been made to completely close this artery to traffic and to continue with the excavations, a fascinating project and a tough challenge which would make this zone one of the most precious archeological sites in the world.

Julius Caesar's Forum was the first of the so-called «Imperial Forums», built using the spoils from the victories of the Gallic wars. On August 9, 48 B.C., the decisive battle was fought at Pharsalus between Caesar's formidable army, triumphantly returning from Gaul, and that of his rival Pompey, who was contesting his primacy in what was already by then the dying Roman Republic. Victorious once again, Caesar built a new forum between the old Republican Forum (which had become too small), and the Quirinal, with the **Temple to Venus Genetrix** in the centre. The Julia family to which Caesar belonged, in fact boasted their descent from Julius or Ascanius, the son of the Trojan hero Aeneas, who, according to Homeric mythology, was born to the mortal Anchises and the goddess Venus. Many art works were collected in the temple, including the statue of Venus Genetrix sculpted by Arcileus who was one of the most celebrated Greek sculptors, and a portrait of Cleopatra. The Temple was rebuilt by Trajan and inaugurated, together with Trajan's column, on May 12, 113.

TRAJAN'S FORUM. The Emperor M. Ulpius Trajan was born in Italica (Spain) in 53 B.C. The formidable task accomplished in his reign was the conquest of Dacia (present day Romania). In 101 he began his campaign: when the roads and forfitications were ready, Trajan took the capital by force and imposed impossibly hard conditions which Decebalus, the leader of the Dacians, did not choose to abide by. In 105 fighting was resumed. The Dacians fought desperately: «to victory or to death»; but their army was wiped out. Their heroic prince committed suicide and Trajan returned to Rome laden with treasures. After the celebrations of his triumph, he wished to remember his victory and decided to build a forum which would surpass all others in size and splendour. He entrusted this task to the great architect Apollodorus of Damascus. The new forum became the most admired place in the city. There were two libraries, a commemorative column, a basilica, a temple, a great equestrian statue of Trajan and a triumphal arch: there was a profusion of statues and groups. Towards the middle of the 4th century, the Emperor Constantius of the East visited Rome, accompanied by the Persian Prince Orsmida. When they reached Trajan's Forum, he was so astonished at the sight of the incredible creation that he exclaimed: «It would be impossible for me even to try to imitate it; at most I would be able to make the horse!». And the Prince observed: «Your Majesty, for such a horse, you would first need a stable like that!».

But the great monument of the Dacian War is the noble **column** that still rises in its pristine majesty, bathed in the glory of more than nineteen centuries.

The BASILICA of S. MARIA D'ARACOELI and the CAPITOL.

The inside of Basilica.

The ashes of the Emperor were placed at the foot of the monument and his statue on top of it. The column consists of 19 blocks of marble and a spiral staircase leads to the top. The most important part of this historic monument is the helicoidal band of figures going all around it which gives us a documentary view of the arms, arts and costumes of both the Romans and the Dacians. Here we see the bridges Trajan built, the forts he attacked, the camps he destroyed, the enemy he put to flight. The old interpretations of the inscriptions on the column have now been recognized as exact. The column shows how deep an excavation was dug to make room for the Ulpia Basilica. This is also shown by the writings of Dion Cassius, who says that the ground was hilly and uneven and Trajan had it levelled even with the top of the column.

Very little remains of the great buildings which surrounded the Column, the **Basilica Ulpia**, destined for the administration of justice, the two libraries Greek and Latin and the temple dedicated to Trajan himself. Besides the wear and tear of the years, the wide stretch of the adjacent Via dei Fori Imperiali which was made in 1932-1933, conceals a large part of this Forum from our sight.

A panoramic view of Rome from the Victor Emmanuel Memorial, Via del Corso, one of Rome's most central streets joining PIAZZA VENEZIA and Piazza del Popolo, can be seen in the background.

The MONUMENT TO VICTOR EMMANUEL II (or «Vittoriano»), designed by Sacconi, was erected to celebrate Italian independence.

The complex of Trajan's markets was erected on the face of the Quirinal hill which was cut through to build the Forum. The two groups of which it consists, a lower construction framed by a semi-circle on three floors, extremely well preserved, and an upper one which contains a large vaulted hall as well as other rooms, which resembles a basilica. These buildings form a marvellous group in which their archeological merits blend with the landscape, making them a real pleasure to the eye. The well preserved state of this complex makes it ideal for exhibitions and cultural events. The entrance is at the side, through a gate opening on to Via IV Novembre, which can be reached up the steps from Via Magnanapoli.

The Forum of Augustus. After Caesar's assassination, Brutus and Cassius, the main culprits, went to the East to take possession of the provinces of Syria and Macedonia. In 42 B.C. they led their armies into battle at Philippi, against the heirs of Caesar, Octavian and Marcus Aurelius. And just as Julius Caesar had taken a vow at Pharsalus, so Augustus took one at Philippi: in the event of victory, he was to dedicate a temple

15

to Mars, the father of the Roman people, in a new forum. After the victory and the death of the two conspirators, Augustus maintained his vow and in the centre of the Forum, he built the **Temple of Mars Ultor** (the Conqueror), in the centre of the new Forum, dedicated to him and inaugurated on the first day of the month of August, in the year 2 B.C. The excavations have brought to light magnificent remains of this Forum and the gigantic temple, which Ovid described. Augustus was the first of the emperors (30 B.C. - 14 A.D.). During his reign, Jesus Christ was born.

The Forum of Nerva. Began by the Emperor Domitian, this Forum was inaugurated in 97 A.D. by his successor Nerva after whom it is called. Built after the Forums of Caesar and Augustus, it was necessary to make the best of a rather limited space, and so it extended in length rather than in breadth. This was the site of the **Temple of Minerva,** which was still standing until 1606 when Pope Paul V had it demolished in order to use its marble for building the Pauline fountain on the Janiculum.

The Temple of Peace. The complex of the Imperial Forums ended towards the Colosseum, with this temple of enormous proportions. Several remains have been found close to the current side-entrance of the Roman Forum, in the gardens in front of the Basilica of Maxentius, and in the Church of St. Cosmos and St. Damian.

At the end of the Via dei Fori Imperiali stands the * **COLOSSEUM,** one of the greatest marvels of the Roman civilization.
This immense amphitheatre, whose ancient splendour we can still admire, was begun by Vespasian in A.D. 72 and finished by his son Titus in A.D. 80. Hebrew prisoners were employed in its construction. Its real name is the **Flavian Amphitheatre,** commonly called Colosseum perhaps because the Colossus of Nero was in its vicinity. There is scarcely a page of Roman history that is not connected with the Colosseum, which became the symbol of the city and its life. Thus in the 8th century the Venerable Bede said: «While the Colosseum stands, Rome shall stand; when the Colosseum falls, Rome shall fall; and when Rome falls, with it the World shall fall». After the sacking of the Normans (1084), nothing but a skeleton remained of antique classic Rome; the Colosseum was abandoned and for years it was used as a quarry for building material. To save what was left of it, Benedict XIV (1740-1758) consecrated the ancient amphitheatre by setting up a permanent **Way of the Cross** and erecting a cross on this site, which the pius legend has linked with the name of the thousands of martyrs who gave up their lives for their faith. In fact, there is no historical proof that Christian massacres took place here even though many Christians were certainly among those who were put to death in this monument. The «Ludi Circenses» were the favourite shows of the Romans, games that were probably invented in the last days of the Republic, with the intention of developing the war-like spirit that had made them the conquerors of the world. This was the origin of the professional gladiators, who were trained to fight to the death, while wild beasts of every sort increased the horror of the show. Dion Cassius says that 9000 wild animals were killed during the hundred days of festivity to celebrate the dedication of this building. After the animals were killed, and removed, the arena was often filled with water in order to stage naval battles. The great Emperor Constantine and his successors tried to stop the gladiatorial fights, but at first the Romans would not give up their customary shows. The last of these events about which we have some evidence, dates back to 523, when Theodoric, King of the Goths, agreed to an animal hunt requested by the consul elected for that year.
The Colosseum, of elliptical form, is 205 yards in its longest diameter and 170 yards in its shortest. On the outside there were three rows of arches, respectively adorned with Doric, Ionic and Corinthian columns, and a fourth floor was adorned with Corinthian pilasters. An ellipse of 80 arches formed the outer circuit. Four arches corresponding to the four semi-diameters, led to a large corridor that went all around it. In the centre of one side of the podium called «suggestum», was the Emperor's seat; the rest of the podium

TRAJAN'S FORUM was erected by the Emperor to celebrate his victory over the Dacians. This grandiose construction is the work of the architect Apollodorus of Damascus.

THE COLOSSEUM - Past and present.   *Inside of the Colosseum - The subterranean.*

was occupied by senators and patricians. Then there were the places for cavaliers, civil and military tribunes. There were also special places for married people, for young men accompanied by their tutors, for families and servants, for women and for the plebeians. The Colosseum was normally uncovered; but in the case of rain or during very hot days it was protected by an immense velarium, which was fixed by two squads of sailors belonging to the fleets of Ravenna and Cape Misenum. These two teams also took part in naval battles, which are however soon moved to suitable pools close to the Tiber. Among them, the «Naumachia Vaticana» is famous. It was designed by Domitian himself, who was responsible for completing the Colosseum.

When the amphitheatre was at the climax of its glory, it must have been a stupendous sight of Roman splendour. But even to-day, after so many centuries, the Colosseum is the pride of Rome and the marvel of visitors.

Between the Colosseum, the Arch of Constantine and the south entrance to the Roman Forum, inte-

A view of the inside of the Amphitheatre during the famous "LUDI CIRCENSES" (Circus Games).

resting excavations have been carried out, which have not only made it possible to replace well known monuments in their original locations, (at least ideally), such as the fountain of the **Meta Sudans** and the base of the «Colossos of Nero», but have supplied numerous clues as to the way this area, including the complex of the **Domus Aurea** (Nero's Golden House), was organized. Before the rule of Nero, a district of rather small, irregular dwellings existed here, whose remains show the clearest traces of the fire of 64 A.D. After this dramatic event, Nero had an artificial lake made in this little valley, in the exact spot which was later occupied by the Colosseum.

The **Arch of Constantine** was erected by the Senate and the Roman people at the extreme limit of the Forum on the Via Sacra, in memory of the victory of Costaintine at Ponte Milvio in 312. Almost all the material was taken from the arches of Trajan and Marcus Aurelius and from other monuments, so that this work may be considered «a true museum of official Roman sculpture, perhaps the richiest and the most important of

The inside of the Colosseum as it is today.

An AERIAL VIEW OF THE COLOSSEUM. Note the extent of its surface when compared to the surrounding houses.

all» (F. Coarelli). From the historical point of view, the most interesting part of the arch is its inscription: «To the Emperor Caesar Flavius Constantine Maximus, "pius, felix, augustus", the Senate and the people of Rome dedicate this notable arch in honour of his triumphs, because, by Divine inspiration and greatness of mind, he freed the Republic by just wars from tyranny and from factions». Now the magistrates of the city were pagans and they knew that Constantine, if not a Christian, favoured Christianity. They did not want to name Christ on a public monument and yet they did not want to offend the Emperor by naming pagan gods. So they found a way to satisfy both sided by saying «Divine inspiration» (to promote divinity). The finest religious buil-

ding in Rome was the twin **Temple of Venus and Roma** of which the ruins still remain.

The columns, scattered on the ground, and now reconstructed and erected on the same spot, give us the idea of the portico that surrounded the temple. It was designed by Hadrian, who had the Colossus of Nero removed to obtain the necessary space.

On the ruins of the Temple of Venus and Roma, was built, in the VII century, the church of «Santa Maria Nova», dedicated at the beginning of the XVIII century to **Santa Francesca Romana.**

The Church is within the precinct of the * **ROMAN FORUM,** the monumental complex whose remains lie between the Capitol, the Impe-

Aerial view of the Roman Forum and of the Colosseum.

rial Forums, the Colosseum and the Palatine.

The centre of the civic and economic life of Rome in the Republican era, the Forum kept its prominent role even in the Imperial age. With the fall of the Roman Empire in the west, however, it fell into a decline, one of whose major causes was the consequence of the disastrous earthquake of 851, during the papacy of Leo IV. The decisive blow was the devastating fury of the Normans who, although they came to Rome ostensibly to help Pope Gregory VII in 1084, as we have seen, set fire to the city and sacked it.

In the following centuries, like the Colosseum, the Forum provided precious marbles and building materials for the families of the great Roman princes. Its remains were gradually buried, and on the hidden ruins of ancient Rome a popular cattle market came to exist which did such a roaring trade that the Forum became known as the «Campo Vaccino» (Cattle Field). Subsequently, the first archeological endeavours at the end of the 18th century and the systematic excavations initiated at the end of the last century which are still progressing today, have made the Forum one of the most sensational archeological sites in the world.

The Forum was crossed by the **Via Sacra** which led to the Capitoline hill and was the route of the triumphal processions of victorious generals, laden with booty and followed by their victoriaus ranks of prisoners. While the most ancient section of the Forum, in the Republican epoch, stretched from the opposite side of the valley to the slopes of the Capitol, the entrance on the square of the Colosseum leads to the most recently built section, which dates from the Imperial age.

Another important street, the **Via Nova,** crossed the length of the valley along the slopes of the Palatine. In this area, until recently little explored, extremely interesting escavations are presently underway which show how, in the very heart of archeological Rome, it is still possible to make unexpected discoveries capable of shedding new light on our knowledge. The zone was largely built up after the death of Nero who had integrated this area into the grounds of his Golden House, at the request of the Emperor Vespasian,

who made it, as we would say today, a real focal point of the city. On the adjacent northern slopes of the Palatine, excavations have revealed a series of private dwellings from the Republican age, including the house of Cicero, who left us precise literary evidence describing this area as «pulcherrimus» (very beautiful).

But this is not enough. The modern stratigraphic systems used by archeologists under the guidance of Professor Carandini, have enabled us to confirm the sensational discovery of the first walls of the city of Romulus. It is now possible to date these to the 8th century B.C., to that fateful year of 753 which has always been considered the traditional year of the city's foundation.

On the Via Sacra, on the very top of the Velia, the **Arch of Titus**, erected by the Senate after the Emperor's death in memory of the conquest of Jerusalem (70 A.D.), stands elegantly to welcome the visitor. In the interior are two fine bas-reliefs: the Emperor on his triumphal chariot and the procession of Jewish prisoners carrying the famous candelabrum with seven branches.

The immense **Basilica of Maxentius,** also called Constantine's Basilica, is the last edifice bearing the impression of the magnificence of ancient Rome. It was begun by Maxentius and finished after the victory by Constantine. This magnificent 4th century construction, which is thought to have inspired Bramante in his design for the new St. Peter's, has been restored, revealing the part facing the Forum.

This is the lesser northern aisle, with its great apse and powerful vaulted domes which were a source of inspiration to the most admired Renaissance architects.

The **Temple of Antoninus and Faustina** is the best preserved in the Forum. The loss of Faustina embittered the Emperor, who often used to say he would have preferred to live in a desert with her than in a palace without her. After her death, the Emperor deified her and erected this magnificent temple in her honour. This temple was later changed into the church of **San Lorenzo in Miranda.** Pagan temples were frequently converted into Christian churches. Even the ancient Church of **St. Cosma and St. Damian,** was built by Felix

An interplay of light and shadow created by the Colosseum's succession of arches. Further back can be seen the ruins of the TEMPLE OF VENUS AND ROMA.

The ROMAN FORUM, centre of the city's public life in ancient times.

IV in 572, inside the «Templum Sacrae Urbis», which the Emperor Vespasian built in the adjacent «Forum of Peace», or «Vespasian's Forum», mainly hidden under the asphalt of the Via de Fori Imperiali. The vestibule stands on the «Tempietto Rotondo», **Circular Temple of Romulus,** the son of Maxentius (4th century), and still preserves the bronze door with its original look. The «Sepolcretum» or «Archaic Necropolis» dates to the 9th century B.C. Thus we have

penetrated one of the oldest areas of the Forum. In fact, according to legend, the first foundations of the **Temple of Vesta** date from the time of King Numa Pompilio, (8th century B.C.). This is a circular building, whose purpose was to guard the Palladium (the image of Minerva) and other sacred objects brought to Italy, according to the legend, by Aeneas and upon which it was believed the security of the city depended. The Vestals had to keep the fire burning. They were six, chosen from patrician maidens, daughters of free parents. They enjoyed special privileges, but if one broke the vow of chastity, she was buried alive in the Field of Villains. They lived close by in the **House of the Vestal Virgins**, which was almost totally reconstructed by the Emperor Septimius Severus after a fire in 191 A.D., as was the temple to the Goddess. Many statues and inscriptions can still be seen; on one of these, the name of a Vestal Virgin was cancelled, leaving only her initial,

"C"... It is quite likely that it was the Vestal Virgin Claudia, to whom a statue was erected in 364 as «homage to her chastity and deep knowledge of religion». Perhaps her name was cancelled because she converted to Christianity.

The **Temple of Julius Caesar,** that Octavianus erected in memory of his uncle, was begun in B.C. 42 on the spot where the Dictator's body was burned, and consecrated in B.C. 29 at the

The ARCH OF CONSTANTINE, erected by the Roman Senate to commemorate Constantine's victory over Maxentius (313 A.D.).

FORUM

1. Curia
2. Arch of Septimius Severus
3. The Rostra
4. Temple of Vespasian
5. Via Sacra
6. Temple of Saturnus

7. Column of Phocas
8. Basilica Julia
9. Basilica Aemilia
10. Temple of Julius Caesar
11. Temple of Vesta

ROMANUM

12. Temple of Castor and Pollux
13. S. Maria Antiqua
14. Temple of Augustus
15. Temple of Antoninus and Faustina
16. Temple of Romulus
17. Temple of Venus and Roma

18. House of the Vestal Virgins
19. Basilica of Maxentius
20. Colosseum
21. Arch of Titus
22. Palatinum

same time as the Arch of Augustus of which only the foundations remain.

The **Regia**, according to tradition, was the house of Numa Pompilius and, later the residence of the «Pontifex Maximus». On the walls are the «fasti consolari» in sculpture. The inscription is in archaic Latin.

The **Temple of Castor and Pollux,** also called the Temple of the Twins, was erected in B.C. 484 to celebrate the victory of Aulus Postumius over the Latins, in the battle at Lake Regillus. The three columns and part of the cornice, very fine work in Pentelic marble, are of the time of Trajan or Hadrian. — It is related that two young men on two white horses appeared during the battle: they were the twins, Castor and Pollux. They rode to Rome, quenched the thirst of their horses at the **fountain of Juturna,** announcing to the Romans

The Roman Forum. The three columns on the left are the remains of the TEMPLE OF VESPASIAN, those on the right belonged to the TEMPLE OF SATURN.

The Roman Forum. THE ARCH OF SEPTIMIUS SEVERUS was erected in honour of Septimius and his sons, Caracalla and Geta.

the victory of their arms, and then disappeared.

St. Maria Antiqua is one of the oldest Roman basilicas built by transforming an imperial edifice annexed to the Atrium Minervae in the 5th century. The church consists of an atrium, a narthex, three naves and a presbytery. On the walls of the apse, we note the frescoes of the 8th century, greatly deteriorated. The church was buried by a landslide in the 9th century and was only brought to light by the excavations of 1900. — To the right of St. Maria Antiqua are the ruins of the **temple of Augustus.**

The **Basilica Julia,** built according to the wishes of Julius Caesar in the middle of the 1st century B.C., was a grandiose building with five naves, divided into sectors with movable divisions which made it possible for more than one audience to take place at the same time. On the steps, and still visible today there are vestiges of chess squares traced on the marble, a pleasurable passtime for the leisurely.

The **Comitium**, the place where the representatives of the people gathered for public discussions, was also at first the tribunal of Rome. It was here, in the first days of the Republic, that Junius Brutus condemned to death his two sons, who had been denounced for plotting the return of King Tarquinius. Here the beautiful Virginia was stabbed by her father. In this square, the most powerful voices of Rome resounded; Cicero, prince of orators, made his famous speeches of the second and third Catilinaria. Here the head of the great writer and politician was explosed to public view after his assassination. There are many memories here of legendary Roman history. There is more history in this place than in entire kingdoms

The **Rostra**, of which the large platform is still visible, were erected by Caesar in 44 B. C. just before his death. The tribunes from which orators, political men and leaders addressed the crowds were called Rostra. In the Republican era, the tribunes were of wood and were situated in the Comitium. In 338 B. C. it as decorated with the prows of Latin ships captured at the battle of Antium. «Ad rostra!»# became the cry of the Roman people to call a meeting.

In 1899 there was discovered the famous **Lapis Niger** which marked the supposed burial place of Romulus. It is a sepulchral monument of the time of the Kings, on which the most ancient Latin epigraph we have is engraved.

The **Column of Phocas** is the last classical monument in the Forum. At the beginning of the 7th century, Phocas, the Emperor of Byzantium, allowed Pope Boniface IV to change the Pantheon into a Christian church. As a sign of gratitude, the Romans took a beautiful carved column from the portico of some ancient building and set it up here, putting the statue of the Byzantine sovereign on top.

The **Arch of Septimius Severus,** ornate to the point of being over-decorated, was erected in honour of Septimius and his two sons, Caracalla and Geta. The inscription recalls an imperial tragedy: after killing Geta, Caracalla had his brother's name removed.

The **Temple of Saturn** was erected by the Consul Titus Larcius on the 17th of December 498 B.C. It was always used as the public Treasury. The ensigns of the Legions and decrees of the Senate were also kept here. In an underground cell were kept the sacred treasures, among which was the gold for ransom given to Brennus and reclaimed by the valour of Camillus.

The **Temple of Vespasian** was erected by his son, Domitian, in 94 and restored by Septimius Severus. Only three columns remain.

The **Temple of Concord** was built by Furio Camillo the conqueror of the Gauls in 367 B.C., in memory of the agreement made at Monte Sacro by the plebians and the patricians. This was the period when the Senate met to hear the last «catilinaria» of Cicero (63 B.C.).

The **Curia,** founded according to the legend by King Tullius Hostilius, (7th century B.C.) was the seat of the Roman Senate. Successively destroyed and rebuilt and transformed in the Middle ages into a Christian church dedicated to St. Hadrian, in the 1930s it was restored to its original condition by a process which some experts consider to have been over drastic.

The ROMAN FORUM. The white remains of temples and marble palaces recall the ancient splendour of the city.

The Roman Forum is crossed by the SACRED WAY which led up to the Capitol

In the area behind the Curia and the Basilica Emilia, excavations by the municipal archeological authority of Rome in collaboration with the section of ancient topography of Rome's «La Sapienza» University, have led to the discovery of impressive foundations belonging to Nerva's Forum, as well as numerous preceding structures from the Republican era. One of the furnaces was also found in which, throughout the Middle Ages, the precious marbles were charred to reduce them to anonymous building material.

Another historic Roman hill, the **PALATINE,** looks over the Forum, preserving unforgettable memories in the greenery of its luxuriant vegetation. During the Republic, the Patrician families dwelt on the Palatine. Quintus Hortensius, the celebrated orator who emulated Cicero, lived here in a house given him by Augustus. When

Augustus became Emperor, he made his imperial residence on the Palatine. Afterwards Tiberius, Caligula, the Flavii and Septimius Severus built palaces here.

The Palatine was the cradle of Rome. Here, according to legend, Romulus traced the square outline of the first city with a plough; here was the seat of the Kings. Because of this the hill was chosen as the residence of the Caesars and up to Septimius Severus, no Emperor left it.

On entering by the Arch of Titus, turning to the left, we climb on the right the **Clivus Palatinus** and following the stairs on the right, we reach the splendid Villa Farnese with its 16th century pavillion and gardens, supported by the powerful arches of the **Domus Tiberiana.** From the terrace on the left, we descend the steps to the **Area Palatina,** where among other venerable memo-

The Roman Forum. Ruins and columns of the TEMPLE OF THE DIOSCURI.

ries there are the ruins of the temple of the **Magna Mater** with the seated statue of Cibele, fragments of the walls of square Rome, some blocks of tufa supposed to belong to the hut of Romulus and traces of the **Scalae Caci,** the primitive access to the Palatine. In the square, an archaic cistern (6th to 5th century B.C.).

From here we descend to the **House of Livia** or, according to others, of Augustus, a typical example of a patrician house of the last period of the Republic. The mural pictures in Pompeian style that still remain, are very interesting even though much damaged. Keeping to the left, we reach the **cryptoportico** built by Nero to unite the Palatine with the Domus Aurea. Then on the right we climb to the **Palace of the Flavii,** built by Domitian; it was designed by his architect, Rabirius. It is formed on the left by a basilica, aula regia and lararium; in the centre by a peristilium. To the right is a triclinium where we see the ruins of the

pavement and two Nymphaea, one of which is in good condition. Under the pavement there are traces of former constructions.

The **Stadium of Domitian** (175 yards long by 52 yds wide) is surrounded by fragments of porticoes, statues, fountains and on one side, the niche of the Imperial lodge. Then we come to the ruins of the **Baths of Septimius Severus,** a mass of constructions, then to the **Septizonium,** an imposing building whose remains were demolished by Sixtus V. From the Belvedere we enjoy a magnificent panorama.

At the foot of the hill, we see the elliptical form of the **CIRCUS MAXIMUS,** where the horse races took place. It was built under the kings, and more and more enlarged during the Republic and the Empire: under the reign of Constantine, it could contain more than 200.000 spectators.

The FABRICIUS BRIDGE, constructed in 62 B.C., is Rome's most ancient bridge. It joins the Tiberina Island to the banks of the Tiber, here known as Lungotevere Cenci.

THE THEATRE OF MARCELLUS

TIBER ISLAND

ST. PAUL'S BASILICA

E.U.R.

On the left side, at the beginning of via del Teatro di Marcello, a rock rises which is thought to be the famous «Rupe Tarpea», whence the traitress Tarpea was precipitated (8th century B.C.) as subsequently all the other traitors of Rome.

The **Theatre of Marcellus** is the only antique theatre left in Rome. It is a fine edifice, erected by Augustus and dedicated to his sister Octavia's son, Marcellus, who died at the age of twenty two greatly mourned and immortalized by Virgil's poem. Later on, this theatre served as a model for the construction of the Colosseum. We can still admire a part of the exterior curved wall with its double row of Doric and Ionic arches, surmounted on the upper part by the Savelli castle (later of the Orsini), erected by Baldassarre Peruzzi.

We come to the Tiber and see the characteristic **ISOLA TIBERINA** (Tiber Island). On the famous temple of Aesculapius, the Greek god of medicine, once the centre for pilgrimages of sick persons, rises the church of **St. Bartholomew on the Island.**
The **Ponte Fabricio** (Quattro Capi) erected in 62 B.C. still almost intact today, and **Ponte Cestio** (46 B.C.) unite the island to the city. The place occupied today by the Palatine Bridge was formerly the site of the **Ponte Sublicio**, noted for the legend of Horace Cocles.

On the other side we see the **Synagogue**, built in 1904 in Assyro-Babylonian style, with its grey cupola of aluminium.
Behind lies the Ghetto, a neighbourhood where the Jews of Rome were segregated from the 6th century to the last century, and where today many Jews still cling tenaciously to their traditions.
Close to the street of the same name, are the remains of the **Portico of Ottavia** — the mother of Marcellus — which was built for her by her brother Augustus. The propylaea of the portico serves as the atrium of the church of **«Sant'Angelo in Pescheria»** (the name derives from the fish market which was once in front of it), founded in the 8th century.
Let us return to the Via del Teatro di Marcello, where on the site of the ancient **Forum Boarium** (the cattle market), today lies the characteristic **Piazza Bocca della Verità** against its interesting backdrop.

The **House of the Crescenzi** built in the 10th century by the powerful Crescenzi family, is an interesting piece of medieval construction, perhaps a fort guarding the river. Its decorations are formed by ancient fragments from several Roman buildings.
The temple called **Fortuna Virile** was not dedicated to this divinity but rather to Mater Matuta. It dates from the Ist century B.C. and is a fine example of the Greek-Italian architecture of Republican times.

The **Church of San Giorgio in Velabro,** (called after the marshland of that name that once existed here) damaged and neglected over the years, was skilfully restored in 1926 to the sober forms of the 7th century, eliminating its baroque superstructures. The lovely bell-tower and the Ionic portico were buikt in the 12th century.

The ancient Sublicius Bridge, near TIBERINA ISLAND, where the Emperor Otto III. (10th century A.D.) erected the Church of St. Bartholomew on the ruins of the Temple of Aesculapius.

The **Arch of the Argentari,** a curious monument covered with poor reliefs, was erected by the money-changers and shop-keepers of the Forum Boarium to Septimius Severus and Julia Domna, whose portraits are seen on the reliefs.

Opposite is the entrance to the **Cloaca Massima** which once drained the water from the surrounding hills and emptied it into the Tiber. The **Arch of Janus** or («Janus the four-faced») with its quadruple arch was built in Constantine's time as a covered passage in the centre of the cross-roads. It had a purely functional purpose: it served as a meeting place and shelter for local shopkeepers.

St. Mary's in Cosmedin, one of the gems of Medieval Rome, rises on the ruins of a temple, perhaps the temple of Ceres. The picturesque austere interior gives us a clear idea of a primitive church (8th century). The **bell-tower** in Romanesque style, of the 12th century, is one of the most beautifull of its kind in Rome.

To the left of the portico is a marble mask called **Bocca della Verità** (mouth of truth); according to popular belief it was said that any one putting his hand in this mouth and swearing falsely, could not withdraw it.

After following the Aventine embankment of the

The MOUTH OF TRUTH. This marble mask, of which popular tradition preserves an amusing legend, is to be found in the Church of S. Maria in Cosmedin.

Tiber and the Via Marmorata, we find ourselves at the Ostiense Gate, in front of the **Pyramid of Caius Cestius,** known in the Middle Ages as the tomb of Romulus. It was built during the last years of the Republic (1st century B.C.) to hold the ashes of Caius Cestius, Praetor, Tribune and Septemvirate of the Epulos, as the inscriptions recall.

Behind the Pyramid lies the **Non-Catholic Cemetery,** once known as the cemetery of the English where many of the foreigners who so loved Rome were laid to rest from English poets such as Perchy Bysshe Shelley and John Keats to the painter Henry Coleman, responsible for some of

the most famous views of the Roman Campagna (countryside). Antonio Gramsci, intellectual and politician who died after long years of imprisonment under the Fascists, is also buried there.

About 2 kms. away on the Via Ostiense, (once in the heart of the countryside) rises the basilica of **ST. PAUL'S OUTSIDE THE WALLS** (or the Basilica Ostiense), built over the burial place of the Apostle of the Gentiles. The building of the first place of worship over St. Paul's tomb has been attributed to the Emperor Constantine. A larger basilica was erected at the end of the 4th century. In the inscription on the mosaic of the triumphal arch, we read that Theodosius began it. Honorius fini-

The stupendous view of the INSIDE OF THE BASILICA OF ST. PAUL.

The BASILICA OF ST. PAUL OUTSIDE THE WALLS. The richly decorated arches of the quadruple portico and the golden mosaic blend particularly well with the severe statue of St. Paul.

BASILICA OF ST. PAUL. The CLOISTER by VASSALLETTO.

shed it and under Leo I (440-461), Placidia restored and decorated it. This splendid basilica, one of the wonders of the world, was destroyed by fire in 1823. Rebuilt on the same foundations and according to the ancient design, the new Basilica was consecrated in 1854 by Pius IX.

The magnificent **four-sided portico** consisting of 150 columns with the majestic statue of St. Paul in the centre, was made by Guglielmo Calderini between 1892 and 1928.

The upper part of the **facade** covered in glittering mosaics by Filippo Agricola and Nicola Consoni, which represent **Christ giving his blessing,** the **Lamb of God, Saints** and **Prophets.** In the narthex, among other things is the bronze central door by Maraini, with its silver damascene work (1930).

The **interior of the basilica,** consisting of one nave and four aisles, is sumptuous and impressive: the eye is enchanted by the endless rows of columns, the mysticlight from the double row of alabaster windows above them, the magnificent white and gold ceiling in Renaissance style, the shining marble pavement, reflecting the light and under the chancel arch the delightful canopy against the background of the gold mosaics of the apse. Between the windows and the columns, is a long sequence of medallions portraying the uninterrupted series of popes from St. Peter to the present day.

On the inner side of the facade, are six alabaster columns that were presented to Pope Gregory XVI after the fire by the Viceroy of Egypt, as a contribution to its rebuilding.

The mosaics of the **chancel arch** date from the 5th century. They were executed by order of the Empress Galla Placidia. After they were damagedby fire in 1823, they were carefully taken down and not too well restored. Later they were put up again and now form one of the glories of the basilica.

The **canopy**, in Gothic style, raised on four columns of porphyry, admirable in harmony of line, is the unsurpassable work of Arnolfo di Cambio (13th century).

The **Cosmatesque cloister**, by Vassalletto, restored in 1907, revealing the ancient roof, must be considered one of the most noteworthy works of Roman marble sculptors, a real masterpiece for the elegant moulding, the richness and the elegance of its mosaics and its carving.

The **façade** on via Ostiense, and the bell-tower, are by Luigi Poletti (1850).

Continuing towards the sea, after several kilometres the Via Ostiense and the Via del Mare, run along the edge of the **EUR.** This is an ultra-modern residential quarter planned at the end of the '30s as the site for a universal exhibition, which was unable to take place because of the outbreak of the 2nd World War. Although it has the typical dramatic features of fascist architecture, this neighbourhood's urban plan is pleasantly spacious and infinitely superior to other sprawling suburban developments which have sprung up over the last ten years in the outskirts of Rome.

EUR. PALAZZO DELLA CIVILTÀ E DEL LAVORO. This modern building, on account of its form and its 216 arches, is often referred to as the "square Colosseum".

QUIRINAL

VIA VENETO

DIOCLETIAN BATHS

ST. MARY MAJOR

The **QUIRINAL** is so called from Quirinus, the Sabine name of the God Mars who was from remote times venerated on this hill, where, under Titus Tatius, the Sabines had emigrated. At the end of the Republic, Quirinus became identified with Romulus, son of Mars.

The immense **Quirinal Palace,** begun by Gregory XIII in 1547, was the Summer residence of the Popes until 1870. Then it became the residence of the King. Now the President of the Republic lives there.

The **beautiful Fountain,** (a granite basin which originally came from the Roman Forum), was moved to the square in 1818 by Raffaele Stern to support the obelisk from the Mausoleum of Augustus and the Statue of the heavenly twins, Castor and Pollux.

On the right, the elegant and majestic **Palace of the Consulta,** by Fuga.

Descending the steep via Quattro Fontane we find on the right the **Barberini Palace** begun under Urban VII to a design by Maderno and continued by Borromini and Bernini until 1640.

It is now the seat of the **National Gallery of Rome.** Among the many paintings exhibited, ranging from the 12th to the 16th centuries, there are some which have acquired world fame, such as * **Fornarina** by Raphael, **Christ and the Adulteress** by Tintoretto, a **Madonna with the Holy Child** by Simone Martini, Fra Angelico's triptych with the **Ascension, Pentecost,** and the **Last Judgment.**

At the end of the slope we reach the **Piazza**

Barberini with the very original **Fountain of the Triton** by Bernini.

We cross it diagonally to reach the aristocratic **VIA VENETO.** At the beginning, on the right, is the **fountain of the Bees,** by Bernini and then the **Capuchin Church** with St. Michael by Guido Reni and the Ecstasy of St. Francis, by Domenichino. Underneath the church, is the **Cemetery of the Capuchins.**

In Piazza S. Bernardo at the end of Via Barberini, is the **Fountain of Moses,** which was commissioned by Sixtus V. The architect, Domenico Fontana had to overcome various difficulties but finally in 1587 succeeded in bringing the «Acqua Felice» to Rome from Colonna.

The modern **Esedra,** today called the Piazza della Repubblica, occupies the place of the ancient exedra which was part of the colossal **Diocletian Baths** complex. In the centre is the great **Fountain of the Naiads** by Rutelli, which was completed in 1911.

The impressive ruins of the Baths which in antiquity surpassed all others in size and splendour, are still evidence of their grandeur and magnificence. They were built in 303.

One of the largest halls in the Baths was transformed into a church by Michelangelo between 1563 and 1566. Originally, the entrance should have opened on to what is now the Piazza dei Cinquecento, but in the 18th century, Luigi Vanvitelli made various changes, including moving the entrance to where it is today. This church is called **St. Mary of the Angels.**

A typical Roman carriage, locally known as «botticella», near the PINCINE GATE at the top end of Via Veneto.
Villa Borghese, Rome's most magnificent park, can be seen behind the gate.

VIA VITTORIO VENETO is famous throughout the world for its elegance: it is also regarded as the drawing room of Roman and international high society. Its coffee houses and hotels are among the most elegant to be found in the city.

The transept, which was designed as the central nave by Michelangelo, is supported by eight enormous, monolithic columns of Egyptian granite, taken from the ancient Baths. When he came to rebuild it in the 17th century, Vanvitelli added the same number of columns in masonry, imitating the granite. The apse was also added by Vanvitelli, halving the wide pool of the Baths, which had remained intact until then.

At the back of the neighbouring Piazza dei Cinquecento, is the modern facade of the main railway station, **Stazione Termini** which was finished in 1950. It is characterized by the bold station roof, popularly called the «dinosaur» because of its vast, ribbed, undulating dimensions which echo the line of the very ancient section of the wall of Servius Tullius which runs parallel.

On the same enormous square, is the entrance to the **NATIONAL MUSEUM OF THE BATHS**, which was inaugurated in 1889. It possesses one of the most precious archeological heritages in the whole world, consisting of finds made in Rome and Lazio towards the end of the past century as well as of the valuable collections of Roman patrician families.

ST. MARY MAJOR is the greatest of many other churches dedicated to Our Lady; it is the

The elegant FOUNTAIN OF THE NAIADS in Republic Square. The white marble of the facade of the Termini Station can be seen in the background.

One of the four splendid nymphs of the Fountain of the Naiads.

only Roman basilica which, in spite of several additional decorations, has preserved its original shape and character.

The basilica, also called «Liberiana», dates from the time of Sixtus III (432-440).

The **façade,** by Fuga, is pleasing. It has a porch with five portals, divided by pillars, adorned by columns and with a loggia above it, with three large arcades. Towering above it is the tallest belfry in Rome, built in Romanesque style. The **interior**, formed by a nave and two aisles, is a magnificent sight. At the end of a double row of columns, under the chancel arch, is the great **canopy** by Fuga, sustained by four precious columns of porphyry.

The **ceiling,** by Julian Sangallo, was gilded according to tradition with the first gold brought from America. Along the architrave a series of thirty-six mosaics, reproducing scenes of the Old Testament is connected with those of the **chancel arch** that showing scenes of the New Testament. All these mosaics are of the 5th century and are of exceptional importance and beauty. The pavement of the basilica is very fine cosmatesque work.

The **Confession** in front of the high altar was decorated in 1874 by Vespignani, who used the richest and rarest marbles. Behind the metal grill are the celebrated relics of the Crib, consisting of five pieces of the Manger in which the Christ-child was placed at his birth, enclosed in a silver urn designed by Valadier. Opposite is the large kneeling **Statue of Pius IX,** by Jacometti.

The **High altar** under the great canopy is the sarcophagus containing the bones of Matthew, the Evangelist. In the apse with ogival windows we admire the **Triumph of Mary,** a fine mosaic by I. Turriti (1295).

The FOUNTAIN OF THE TRITON, in Piazza Barberini.

*The FOUNTAIN OF THE NAIADS
and the Church of St. Mary of the Angels.*

The BASILICA OF S.
MARIA MAGGIORE
is the only church to
have kept intact its
form of an early
Christian church.
The facade is work
of the Fuga.

ST. PETER IN CHAINS

COLLE OPPIO

ST. CLEMENT

ST. JOHN IN LATERAN

The basilica of **ST. PIETRO IN VINCOLI** (St. Peter in Chains) was due to the generosity of an Imperial matron, Eudoxia, daughter of Theodosius the Young, and wife of Valentinian III. Her mother had sent her the chains jused by Herod to chain Peter which she had received from Juvenal, bishop of Jerusalem. To preserve these chains, young Eudoxia erected this basilica, then called «Eudoxiana», but to-day commonly known as «St. Peter in Chains».

The nave is divided by twenty columns taken from an old monument.

To the left of the entrance is the **Tomb of Anthony Pollaiolo** (1432-1498), sculptor, jeweller, painter, engraver, who settled in Rome in 1489, where he did many works, among which the large monument to Sixtus IV that is now in the new Museum Petriano. His brother who helped him, is also buried here.

Every one comes to this church to see the celebrated * **Statue of Moses,** with which the gigantic genius of Michelangelo brought Renaissance sculpture to the apex of magnificence. This austere chief of his own people, this just legislator who was accustomed to speak with God, is seated here, still radiant with the sight of God, with such an air of biblical majesty, that nobody can help being dominated in his senses and penetrated to the very depths of his soul.

In 1505 the artist was called to Rome by Julius II who wanted him to make a Mausoleum for himself worthy of ancient Rome: but he suddenly changed his mind. He thought that a new St. Peter's would be better than a Mausoleum, to perpetuate his glory.

The monument was built, as we see it today, under Paul II (1534-1549). Very little remains the glorious dream of its great architect. The two statues of **Rachel and Leah,** symbolizing the active and the contemplative life were designed by Michelangelo, but everything else was the work of his pupils.

In the **COLLE OPPIO** is the access to the celebrated «Domus Aurea», of Nero, an imposing, fantastic group of buildings that extended from the Palatine to the Esquiline, submerged in the greenery of a countryside recreated within the city, occupying an extensive area. However, of so many marvels, almost everything disappeared instantly after the death of Nero. His successors wanted to eradicate the slightest memory of these achievements, whose luxury had aroused passionate hatred in Roman hearts. This was the site of the central pavilion, ruined in 104 by a terrible fire. Over it were built the foundations for the construction of the **Baths of Trajan,** of which only a few ruins remain.

The **BASILICA OF ST. CLEMENT,** mentioned by St. Jerome in the 4th century, is one of the most interesting in Rome from an artistic and archeological point of view. It was almost buried under the enormous quantity of debris accumulated in that zone after the terrible fire caused by the Normans in 1084, but was rebuilt in the 12th century by Paschal II on a higher level. The new

The Tomb of Pope Julius II, the work of Michelangelo. The Pope, a member of the della Rovere family, commissioned the tomb during his lifetime. The centrepiece of the tomb is constituted by the powerful and majestic figure of MOSES, leader of the Jewish people.

basilica was built in the original form with all the architectural elements it was possible to save, so that it remains, in spite of restorations and modification of more recent date, a rare example of a typical early Christian basilica.

There are notable works of art of the Renaissance in this basilica. In the first chapel of the left aisle, we admire the famous frescoes of Masolino da Panicale (1431), formery attributed to Masaccio. In the centre to the left, St. Christopher; on the central wall, a dramatic Crucifixion; on the later walls, to the right, episodes from the life of St. Ambrose, and St. Catherine, to the left. On the altar a Madonna, by Sassoferrato. In the chapel at the end of the nave, the Madonna of the Rosary by Sebastian Conca. Further on in front of the last arch, the Tomb of Cardinal Venerio whose columns belonged to the original canopy. In the right aisle, besides the Tomb of Archbishop Brusati, by L. Capponi (1485), is the Monument to Cardinal Roverella, his uncle, a fine work by A. Bregno and G. Dalmata.

Now we are on the square of St. John in the Lateran. In front of the Basilica's side facade, the **obelisk of the Lateran** rises, the highest of the thirteen which were erected in the squares of Rome. It was made in 1449 B.C. by Totmes III

The famous CHAINS with which St. Peter was imprisioned during the reign of Herod are conserved in this bronze urn.

The so-called «FONTANA DELLA NAVICELLA», a fountain reproducing an ancient Roman ship. Behind it can be seen the entrance to the Church of S. Maria in Domnica.

and his son Totmes IV of the XVIII dynasty of the Pharaohs and transported in the 4th century to Rome, where it was set up in the Circus Maximus. Sictus V had it re-erected here by Fontana (1588).

The **LATERAN** was the residence of the Popes up to 1305 i.e. until they moved from Rome to Avignon. Their palace, the «Patriarchium», was pulled down in 1596 by Domenico Fontana by command of Pope Sixtus V, who ordered the present one to be built.

On the right of the square is the **Baptistery.** It was erected by the Emperor Constantine where,

according to an erroneous tradition, he had been christened by Saint Silvester. Later on, it was rebuilt by order of Sixtus III (432-440) and afterwards several popes had it restored. It is an octagonal structure. Eight columns of porphyry sustain the cornice and another eight of marble the dome.

To the left of the square is the **Scala Santa.** According to tradition it is the same flight of marbles steps which Jesus ascended in the house of Pilate; it was brought to Rome by the pious Empress Helena. The twenty-eight steps may only be ascended kneeling. At the top of the stairs

55

is the private chapel of the Popes which formed a part of old Patriarchium, called the «Sancta Sanctorum», richly decorated by Cosmati in 1278. At the sides of staircase are two splendid groups by Jacometti: the «Kiss of Judas», and «Pilate showing Christ to the People».

St. JOHN IN THE LATERAN is the Cathedral of Rome, the mother of all churches in Rome and in the world. Founded by Constantine and called the «Basilica of the Saviour» during the time of Silvester (314-335) it has been destroyed and rebuilt many times. The actual basilica dates from the 17th century.

The imposing **façade** in travertine was constructed in 1735 by Alexander Galilei, who used all his architectural ability on the portico. To the left we see a **Statue of Constantine** which was found at the Quirinal; a poor statue, showing the decadence of art at that time. The **bronze doors** were taken from the Curia in the Forum, by Alexander VII (1655-1667).

The **inside,** with its five aisles, retains little of the ancient mediaeval basilica; the same antique columns of granite were covered by pilasters by Borromini in the course of the radical reconstruction which was carried out in the mid-17th century. Against the new pilasters, the artist arranged twelve imposing **tabernacles** each with two ancient green marble columns, which came from the old Basilica. The **statues of the Apostles** all round the nave, are of the Bernini school. The **bas-reliefs** are among the most important works of Algardi (1603-54), the Caracci of sculpture. The **ceiling** is the superb work of F. Boulanger and Vico di Raffaele. The pavement is cosmatesque. Underneath it were found notable remains of ancient constructions.

The **lateral aisles** were totally rebuilt by Borromini, with a rhythmic succession of arches in the intermediate aisles and architraves in the outer aisles, which give it a new spirit, original and vigorous.
The many funeral monuments already in existance were reorganized in baroque aediculae by Borromini, who had no qualms about dismantling

them when he felt it was necessary, with a decisiveness which would cause a scandal today.

At the third pillar, is **the monument to Alexander III** (1159)-1181) who led the fight against Frederic Barbarossa (1123-1190). In 1166 the Emperor besieged the Vatican, after devastating various territories of Italy. The Pope mobilized the Lombardy League against him, an alliance of Italian municipalities. They erected the fortress of Alessandria, which received this name in honour of the Pope. After the Italian victory in Legnano, negotiations began which ended with the Peace Treaty of Venice, where the proud Emperor knelt to kiss the Pope's foot. In the centre of the transept, is the **Papal Altar,** surmounted by a canopy supported by four columns, built in 1367 by Urban V (136"-1370). Beneath it, can be seen a bronze plaque: the splendid work of Simone, Donatello's brother; on this is sculpted the recumbent figure of **Martin V** (1417-1431) remembered in the inscription as «temporum suorum felicitas» (the happiness of his times).

Leo XIII ordered the architect Vespignani to extend the apse. The transfer of the *****Mosaic of the Redeemer** was ably executed and this venerable work was also restored. It dates back to the first building of the Basilica (4th century) and was restored for the first time in 1291 almost a thousand years later, by Jacopo Torriti and Jacopo da Camerino. Hig up, it shows the smiling face of the Redeemer giving his blessing, which appeared, according to legend, on the apse of the Basilica as soon as it was built, thus sanctioning the sublime rite with his divine presence.

The **Papal throne** below, which in this Basilica, the Cathedral of Rome, is also the bishops' throne, is made of precious marbles studded with dazzling mosaics.

To the left of the Tribune, the splendid **Monument to Leo XIII**, noble work of Tadolini. Leo XIII, one of the greatest modern Popes, was buried here in October 1924. In this monument, Tadolini combined the Renaissance style with the modern. The statue on the left, a workman, reminds

THE HOLY STAIRCASE. Tradition has it that Jesus climbed this staircase in the house of Pontius Pilate. The staircase was later brought to Rome by the pious Empress Helen, mother of Constantine the Great.

us of the encyclical «Rerum Novarum» that was called the Magna Charta of Christian Sociology, in which Leo established the reciprocal relations between workers and employers in the practice of justice and love. Through a door between the left hand aisle and the transept one goes out into the airy **cloister,** the work of famous Roman marble workers of the 13th century, the Vassalletto. It has remained almost intact, and though it is made out of a combination of extremely varied elements, it gives a harmonious impression of unity.

Right in front of the façade of the Basilica, since 1926, is the bronze **Statue of St. Francis,** who raises his arms towards the Lateran Church as he really must have done in front of the Patriarchium when he first met the Pope who ruled the Catholic World. Thus did Innocent III see him in a dream sustaining the imperilled Lateran.

ST. JHON IN LATERAN. The papal sheltered under a canopy was erected by altar Urban V. in 1367.

TORRE ARGENTINA

CAMPO DE' FIORI

JANICULUM

TRASTEVERE

The **Fountain of the Tortoises** in the small Piazza Mattei, is the most charming in Rome. Its beauty and its fine lines gave birth to the legend that this artistic jewel of the late 16th century was designed by Raphael; in reality, it is the work of Landini (1585).

Four **Republican Temples** not impressive in size but interesting and very ancient, have come to light in the monumental zone of largo Torre Argentina.

S. Andrea della Valle was built, on the design of C. Maderno, from 1591 to 1650. The dome, the highest in Rome after St. Peter's, is also one of the finest. The façade of travertine is an impressive work by Rainaldi.

The interior forms a Latin cross. The ample nave, wide, beautiful and full of light, the large side chapels, the apse, the ceiling and dome all combine to give an impression of splendour and solemnity.

The **Campo de' Fiori** is the place where for a long time capital punishment took place. Here on February 17th 1600, the philosopher Giordano Bruno, who escaped punishment in Switzerland, Bohemia and England, was burned as a heretic. The monument is the fine work of Ettore Ferrari.

And now, after crossing the Ponte Amedeo di Savoia, we go up to the **JANICULUM,** from where there is a most varied and attractive view of the Eternal City. At the end of the slope of Sant'Onofrio we enter the villa, where the beautiful «Passeggiata of the Gianicolo» running all round the hill, begins.

On the right, in the **Church of St. Onophrius,** stands the **Monument to Torquato Tasso**, a work by De Fabris, erected by order of Pope Pius IX two and a half centuries after the poet's death. Proceeding along the slope, amid a group of cypresses we come across the historical ruin of **Tasso's oak,** beneath which the poet loved to sit in the shade and where San Filippo Neri gathered many young boys in order to teach them by amusing them.

Further on, we reach the **Lighthouse,** a symbol of the Italian spirit of Rome; from its small terrace we admire the first panorama of the «passeggiata».

Still further, on the left, there is the 16th century **Lante Pavillion** and on the right we see the **Monument to Anita Garibaldi,** a splendid work by M. Rutelli (1932). Still further, we reach the large terrace of the Gianicolo on which stands the **Monument to Giuseppe Garibaldi,** a work by E. Gallori (1895).

It is from this terrace that one has the most famous view of the city.

Over the undulating sea of roofs, the numerous domes of Rome are silhouetted against the distant backdrop of an amphitheatre of mountains, white the Tiber with its meanders determines the city's unmistakable shape. The Passeggiata Gianicolense ends in the beautiful avenue bordered by the busts of the patriots of the Roman Republic (1849). On the right of the exit, we see the **Fontana Paolina,** the most splendid fountain in Rome, made by G. Fontana and C. Maderno, erected in 1611 by Paul V who wished to restore the aqueduct constructed by Trajan in the year

The TORTOISES'S FOUNTAIN, one of the many beautiful Baroque fountains to be found in Rome, was designed by Giacomo della Porta and executed by the sculptor Taddeo Landini in 1585.

The best view of the city is enjoyed from the JANICULINE HILL.

109 in order to carry the water from the Braccia-no lake to Rome. The vast semicircular basin was added in 1690 by Carlo Fontana.

Further down, on the left, we come to the church of **San Pietro in Montorio** where Beatrice Cenci (1577-1599) famous for her tragic history, was buried. She was arrested with other members of her family and on September 11th, 1599 they were all executed.

The famous Renaissance architect Bramante built his glorius **Tempietto** in the courtyard of the convent, on the spot where, according to one tradition, St. Peter was crucified.

Following the Via Garibaldi, down the hill from he Janiculum one reaches **Trastevere**, the «heart of Rome» and a very popular district which we hope will keep its character in spite of the changes due to a certain internationalization of this famous part of the city. A detailed visit of this ancient district, rich with old churches and fine buildings, cannot be included in this itinerary due to an obvious lack of space. However, we advise you to end this fascinating walk by wandering through the streets in Trastevere, where you can still get a feeling of the most genuine atmosphere of the city.

THE TREVI FOUNTAIN

TRINITÀ DEI MONTI

VILLA BORGHESE

FORO ITALICO

The **via del Corso** is the principal, most central, and most typical of the old Roman streets. At one end of its narrow but imposingly straight line, nearly a mile long, is the obelisk of the Piazza del Popolo; at the other end, the «Vittoriano». It is bordered with many papal and princely palaces (Salviati, Odescalchi, Sciarra, Marignoli, on the right; Bonaparte, Doria, Chigi, Fiano, Ruspoli, Rondanini, on the left). The name Corso (race) derived from the special horse races that took place there up to the past century: it replaced the ancient «via Lata».

To the right of the Via del Corso, in the Via delle Muratte, is the most sumptuous fountain in Rome: The **FONTANA DI TREVI** is not only celebrated for its excellent water but for the legend that whoever drinks it or throws a coin in the fountain, will assure his return to Rome. It is the façade of a large palace decorated with statues and bas-reliefs on heaps of rocks: the water gushes from every part. It was Agrippa who brought the Virgin Water to Rome by means of an aqueduct. The fountain was built by the architect Salvi (1735) in the time of Clement XII, and decorated by several artists of Bernini's school.
It is said that the soldiers of Agrippa, looking for water in the via Collatina in the country, met a maiden who showed them the source of this pure water, which was hence called Virgin Water. The bas-relief on the right represents this event; that on the left shows Agrippa explaining to Augustus the plan to bring this water to Rome.

A thorough restoration has recently been completed, (1991) which has given it back all its original splendour.

Almost half way down of the Corso is the **Piazza Colonna,** with the Column of Marcus Aurelius. After the death of the Emperor-Philosopher, the Senate erected a temple and a column in his honour. The column was surmounted by a bronze statue of the Emperor.

On the square is the **Chigi Palace**, the Prime Minister's Office. On the opposite side of the Corso is the Colonna Gallery. The **Montecitorio Palace** on the square close by with the same name is the headquarters of the Chamber of Deputies: the old section, Innocent's Palace, was built by Bernini, the newest part was built by Basile, (1650-1694).

Continuing, we come to the Largo Goldoni. From here, by the elegant and famous Via Condotti, we reach the **PIAZZA DI SPAGNA.** The first thing that strikes one is the charming, monumental **flight of steps** (1772) whose sinuous lines harmoniously follow the slope of the hill. At its feet is the graceful **Fountain of the Little Boat** by P. Bernini. On the right, in the next square, Piazza Mignanelli, is the **column of the Immaculate Conception**, a monument erected to commemorate the proclamation of the Dogma (1856).

At the top of the Spanish steps is the Church of the **TRINITA DEI MONTI**, with its two cupolas (1495), and in front of its façade is an obelisk,

63

The monumental TREVI FOUNTAIN, another example of the Baroque style, was constructed by Nicolò Salvi under the pontificate of Clement XII in 1762. He based himself on designs by Alberti and Bernini.

The TREVI FOUNTAIN and its rustling water animate a small square in the centre of Rome, a jowel of 18th century architecture that suddenly and surprisingly presents itself to the visitor's eyes after he has traversed a series of tiny, narrow streets.

wich was taken from the Sallustian gardens in 1789. Inside of the church, the masterpiece of Daniele da Volterra, the famous fresco of the **Descent from the Cross.**

Lying prettily the foot of the steps, at the fine Fountain of the «Barcaccia» by Pietro Bernini, father of the famous sculptor and architect Gian Lorenzo.

PIAZZA DEL POPOLO was designed by Valadier at the turn of the century. It is an enormous square, architecturally superb and perfectly symetrical. In the centre stands the city's second **obelisk,** which was brought to Rome by Augustus, and erected here by Fontana under Sixtus V (1589).

According to the legend, in the early middle ages Nero's spirit haunted this place where his ashes had been deposited in the Domitian family's tomb. This is why the people destroyed the Mausoleum and built a church there, **S. MARIA DEL POPOLO**, one of the most interesting in Rome. It was probably built in the 11th century, but it was completely reconstructed in the early Renaissance.

Among the many works of art to be seen here are: **Adoration of the Child**, by Pinturicchio on the altar of the first chapel on the right; a **Tabernacle** by Andrea Bregno, in the Sacristy; two monuments by Sansovino: to Cardinal della Rovere, on the right, and to Cardinal Sforza, on the left of the high altar. On the ceiling, the **Coronation of the Virgin** and other frescoes by Pinturicchio; two

As soon as one arrives in PIAZZA DI SPAGNA one is struck by the enchanting staircase that leads up to the CHURCH OF TRINITÀ DEI MONTI. In springtime the staircase gives hospitality to an exhibition of azaleas and it then becomes a splendid sea of colour.

masterpieces by Caravaggio: **Saul on the road to Damascus**, on one side, the **Crucifixion of St. Peter,** on the other, in a chapel of the transept on the left. Martin Luther, then an Augustinian friar, lived in the adjoining convent.

The church stands on the lower slopes of the **PINCIO** gardens, designed by Valadier in 1810. There is a **wonderful view** from the hig terrace: in the distance St. Peter's and the Vatican dominated by the Dome of Michelangelo, the largest one ever built, in the most brilliant sky. People come here to admire the famous Roman sunsets.

Now we enter one of the loveliest gardens of Rome, a revelation of what Rome and the greatness of the nobility could do jointly, a garden not to be found elsewhere: the **VILLA BORGHESE.** After the election of Paul V, a Borghese, his young nephew, Scipio, was made Cardinal with a very substantial prebend. The Cardinal ordered to design this splendid Villa, a Paradise of delight, as it was called at the time.

On the highest point of the Villa stands the **Borghese Pavillion**. It was built in 1613 by the Dutch architect van Zans (Vasanzio) and restored

The CHURCH OF TRINITÀ DEI MONTI was erected in 1495 by commission of the French government and intended for the use of French Catholics.

The romantic LAKE IN THE VILLA BORGHESE PARK with its small temple once dedicated to Aesculapius.

in 1782 by order of Marcantonio Borghese. Today it is the home of the **BORGHESE MUSEUM AND GALLERY.**

The same Cardinal Scipione Borghese kept his extremely rich collections of works of art, both sculptures and paintings, in this Pavillion. Towards the end of the 17th century the best pictures were taken from the gallery to the Borghese Palace. One century after this, the museum that in the meantime had been again enriched by Marcantonio Borghese, with new classical sculptures, had to suffer a still more severe spoliation by Camillo Borghese who, being a brother in-law of Napoleon, ceded a large part of his works of art to the Louvre in Paris. The protests of the Papal government were all in vain, and it was necessary to collect new statues and marbles with which Francesco Borghese succeeded in bringing the museum to its present state.

VIA CONDOTTI, a narrow street that leads from Via del Corso to Piazza di Spagna, is undoubtedly one of the most elegant and sophisticated thoroughfares in the city.

The view from the terrace on the Pincine Hill. The foreground is occupied by PIAZZA DEL POPOLO.

The gracious MOSES FOUNTAIN on the Pincine Hill.   *The CLOCK FOUNTAIN on the Pincine Hill.*

Leaving Villa Borghese by Piazzale Flaminio, we admire the **Porta del Popolo** that recalls the entry of Charles V (1536) and of Christine of Sweden.
Via Flaminia starts here; it is one of the ancient Roman consular roads, which went to Rimini on the Adriatic Sea.
Following the Tiber, opposite the Ponte Duca d'Aosta 2 kms away, one reaches the **Italic Forum** a complex of buildings for games and athletic exercises, gymnastics and sports, which includes the **Olympic Stadium** with a capacity of more than 80,000. It was rebuilt, completely covered over and fully equipped with seats for the World Football Championships of 1990.
A few metres away, the ancient **Milvian Bridge,** spans the Tiber. This was the scene of the battle between Maxentius and Constantine, where the latter, having defeated his opponent and replacing the standard with the cross, proceeded triumphantly to Rome on October 28, 312. The bridge, also traditionally called «ponte Molle», dates from the Roman.

The new Olympic Stadium.

MINERVA

THE PANTHEON

NAVONA SQUARE

ST. ANGEL CASTLE

S. MARIA SOPRA MINERVA, the only large Gothic church in Rome, was designed by the Dominican friars who built S. Maria Novella in Florence (1280-1290) and is a real museum of art and history.

Under the high altar, in a marble sarcophagus lies the **Body of St. Catherine of Siena** (1347-1380). Her greatest glory consists in having persuaded the Pope to return to Rome, after the «Babylonian captivity» of the Church had lasted seventy three years. Dante, Petrarch, and many other good Italians attempted it but their efforts were fruitless. Young Catherine tried first by correspondence, then went to Avignon. Gregory XI returned to Rome. Her letters to kings, popes, and other famous people, have great political importance, a spiritual quality and a high literary value. Leo X (1513-1521), the son of Lorenzo the Magnificent, was a great patron of the arts and deserves a prominent position among the popes: artists and intellectuals soon came to know his benevolence. He raised the Church to a high level, because of his love of all that could extend human knowledge or make life beautiful. This is why he also experienced great bitterness. It was in his reign that Luther started the Reformation. On the left of the altar stands the famous **statue of Christ with the cross,** sculpted by Michelangelo between 1514 and 1521.

The **obelisk of Minerva,** in the square of the same name, stood originally in front of the temple of Isis. It was put here by order of Alexander VII in 1667. Bernini whimsically set the obelisk on the back of an elephant, a work of Ferrata, one of his best pupils.

The **PANTHEON,** a glory of the Eternal City, is the most perfect of all classical monuments in Rome. The inscription on the architrave of the portico «M. Agrippa L. F. Cos tertium fecit» refers to a temple erected by Agrippa in 27 B.C. to the tutelary divinities of the Julia Family. For a long time, it was thought that the Pantheon, as it is today, was the original temple of Agrippa. In reality Agrippa's building was destroyed by a great fire in A.D. 80. Recent studies have proved that the present Pantheon is a reconstruction of the time of Hadrian. Other alterations were made at the time of Septimius Severus and of Caracalla. On the 6th March 609, Boniface IV, with the permission of Emperor Phocas, changed the pagan temple into a Christian church dedicating it to St. Mary of the Martyrs. It is to this fact we owe the preservation of the Pantheon. The bodies of many martyrs were removed from the Catacombs to be buried here.

As a sanctuary, in virtue of the Lateran Pact, it acquired the status of palatine basilica or, in other words, of the national church of all Italians.

The **portico** is supported by 16 monolithic granite columns; in the tympanum there was a bas-relief in bronze representing the battle of gods and giants. The ceiling of the portico was covered with bronze. This precious material, weighing about 450.000 lbs, was removed by order of Urban VIII (1623-1644) and used by Bernini for the high altar at St. Peter's and other works. It

The Pantheon by night.

was precisely the removal of the bronze from the ceiling, which inspired Pasquino, the famous «talking statue», to make the «pasquinade» or quip: «What the barbarians did not do, the Barberini did»! In the two niches, statues of Augustus and Agrippa once stood. The **bronze doors** are original.

The **interior** measures 43, 40 metres in diametre, and the same in height. Light and air still enter through the opening at the top (a circle of 8m. 92cms in diametre, which still retains part of the original bronze-covered rim) Heaven itself seems to pour into this temple left open so that prayers could freely ascend. All this gives an impression of unequalled solemnity: its simple regularity, the beauty of its proportions and the splendid materials used, combine to make the interior sublime.

The solemn **dome** is in fact a cap, whose thickness gradually dimishes from the bottom to the top. All around are seven niches. In the centre stood the statue of Jove Ultor who punished the assassins of Caesar; in the others were statues of the chief divinities. Other gods and heroes were in the intermediary spaces. Only the splendid columns of antique yellow marble remain to give us an idea of its primitive splendour.

Sovereigns and artists have their tombs in the Pantheon: in the first chapel to the left repose the

The MINERVA OBELISK, which we here see in the small square in front of the Church of S. Maria sopra Minerva, was designed by Bernini and executed by Ferrata in 1667.

remains of **Perin del Vaga** (1500-1547), considered second only to Giulio Romano among Raphael's pupils.

Next is the **tomb of Baldassarre Peruzzi** (1481-1536), a great painter and architect.
In the second chapel are the **tombs of King Umberto I and Queen Margherita.**

Between the second and third chapels, the tomb that contains the earthly remains of Raphael, one of the most popular artists in the world, whose epigraph says: «Living, great Nature feared he might outlive her works; and dying, fears herself to die». **The Statue of the Madonna** is the work of his pupil Lorenzetto. Close by is the tomb of **Maria Bibbiena,** his promised wife, who died three months before him. Above is the tomb of **Annibale Caracci.** In the third chapel we see the **Cenotaph of Cardinal Consalvi** (1755-1824) an exquisite work by Thorwaldsen.

In the sixth chapel, is the **tomb of Victor Emanuel II.** On the altar of the seventh chapel, a fresco of the Annunciation, by Melozzo da Forlì.

A stone's throw away in the Via della Scrofa, is the Church of **St. Louis of the French,** the national church of the French in Rome. The late Renaissance facade is by Giacomo della Porta.

The INSIDE OF THE PANTHEON has a diameter of 43.40 metres (about 143 ft) and is as high again. Some of Italy's most famous kings and artist are buried here.

PIAZZA NAVONA is one of the largest squares in Rome. It stands above the remains of the Circus of Domitian whose original form it preserves.

Inside, there are superb frescoes by Domenichino in the «Chapel of S. Cecilia», and on the altar is a copy by Guido Reni of **St. Cecilia** by Raphael, whose original is in Bologna. Without a doubt, this church's gems are the wonderful Caravaggio paintings of the **life of Saint Matthew** which were hung here in the St. Matthew chapel in 1600.

The neighbouring **Palazzo Madama**, so called because Margherita Farnese, daughter of Charles V, lived here, houses the Senate of the Italian Republic. Frescoes and fine stuccoes by Maccari and his pupils adorn it. Noteworthy: the blind senator Appius Claudius refusing the peace proposals of Cineas, a messenger of King Pyrrhus; the departure from Ostia of Attilius Regulus for Carthage, where he will meet with torture and death; the solemn assembly of the Roman Senate in the Temple of Concordia to hear the last «Catilinaria» of Cicero.

PIAZZA NAVONA. The FOUNTAIN OF THE FOUR RIVERS (seen by night) is the work of Bernini. Four figures represent the Danube, the Ganges, the Nile and the River Plate.

The **PIAZZA NAVONA**, or Circo Agonale, occupies the place of the Stadium of Domitian, that could hold 30.000 spectators. Here are three magnificent fountains. The one in the centre, «an Aesop's fable fashioned in marble» is the **Fountain of the Four Rivers** by Bernini, who made it as a base for the Egyptian **obelisk** brought here from the Circus of Maxentius.

It contains four statues which represent the Danube, the Ganges, the Nile and the Rio de la Plata.

The church of **S. Agnese in Agone**, is built on the spot where, according to tradition, the virgin, denuded before her martyrdom, was mantled in her hair, which had grown miraculously to cover her. It is a magnificent baroque building designed by G. Rainaldi and Borromini. Beneath it are some remains of the original church and of the Circus of Domitian.

CASTEL SANT'ANGELO. Artemisia, Queen of Halicarnassus, wife of King Mausolus, became immortal through the magnificent tomb, one of the wonders of the world, which she erected for her husband. It was called Mausoleum, and this name has been used ever since for tombs of large dimensions. The **Mausoleum of Hadrian** surpassed in dimensions and magnificence every other tomb. We get no idea of it from what remains. It would require too great an effort of imagination to re-evoke all its splendour. Procopius, the

The FOUNTAIN OF THE FOUR RIVERS in Piazza NAVONA, below its tall central obelisk (an Egiptian original).

The SANT'ANGELO BRIDGE was constructed by the Emperor Hadrian in 134 to give acces to his MAUSOLEUM.
The statues are later additions executed by the school of Bernini.

Byzantine historian of the 6th century, left us a description of it in his time. The Mausoleum had square foundations above which rose a big tower adorned with Doric columns, statues and spaces for epitaphs of the dead. On the top was a colossal group representing Hadrian in a chariot drawn by four horses. All the enormously thick walls were faced with Parian marble. It was, after the Colosseum, the most splendid example of Roman architecture.

At the death of the Emperor, the Mausoleum was not yet finished; his successor Antoninus Pius brought his remains to Rome. His successors and princes of Imperial families were buried here up to Caracalla. The history of Hadrian's Mausoleum follows the history of Rome and both saw the struggles and treachery of the Middle Ages, the splendour of the Papal Court in the Renaissance, the horrors of the Sack of Rome in 1527, the furious bombardments during many sieges, and inoffensive fireworks of festivities. Under Aurelian (275) but more probably under Honorius (403) it was strongly fortified and incorporated in the city walls in order to form a real bastion, in defence of the banks of the Tiber. This strategic function came into evidence in the first invasion of the barbarians led by Alaric in 410. It was probably transformed into a castle in the 10th century, when it fell into the hands of Alberich and his mother, Marozia, powerful figures in Rome at the time, whose alternating fortunes reflect the city's contemporary history. It then passed to the Crescentius and in 1277 it was occupied by Nicholas III who connected it to the Vatican by the famous corridor, a safety passage which runs along the top of the encircling wall of the Vatican. Henceforth, it remained under the control of the Popes who used it as a fortress, to impress, but also as a prison and a place for torture.

Its dedication to the Angel dates from the 12th century, but owes its origin to a legend which is far older. During a solemn procession made in 590 by St. Gregory the Great, to implore the Virgin to put an end to the plague which was devastating the city, an angel appeared in the sky and came to rest on the mausoleum, sheathing his sword as a sign of grace granted. A chapel was subsequently erected in honour of the Angel and later a statue to recall the miracle; the building was then renamed in memory of the event.

The castle is steeped in memories of bloodshed and crime. Famous prisoners were shut up in it. Arnaldo da Brescia, ardent adversary of temporal

Castel S. Angelo - THE COURT-YARD OF THE ANGEL.

A picturesque view of CASTEL SANT'ANGELO.

dominion, was accused by St. Bernard of following the doctrines of Peter Abelard; denounced, he had to leave Paris and came to Rome where he began a campaign against the clargy. In July 1148, Eugene III excommunicated Arnaldo and his followers.

A cardinal was killed and the Pope placed Rome under an interdict. Arnaldo was burned and his ashes thrown into the Tiber.

Clement VII was besieged in this fort, while the city was occupied by invaders led by the Prince of Orange. From the 6th of May to the 3rd of June 1527, the poor Pope from the corridor of the Castle witnessed the horrible saturnalia of blood and licence, theft and sacrilege, in terrible excesses after the Constable of Bourbon entered the city with his ferocius troups (Sack of Rome).

Benvenuto Cellini, the famous Renaissance artist who found himself imprisoned here during the seige, accomplished various services for Clement VII and he himself tells of having beaten the Bourbon to death, and then Philibert, Prince of Orange.

The **Ponte S. Angelo** was built by Hadrian as an approach to his mausoleum. It is decorated with beautiful figures of angels, designed by Gian Lorenzo Bernini and accomplished by his pupils.

THE BATHS OF CARACALLA

THE APPIAN WAY

THE CATACOMBS

TOMB OF CECILIA METELLA

No other road is so well known, in the world as the **Via Appia.** Proudly called the «Regina Viarum», it was begun by Appius Claudius in 312 B.C. Bordering it for many miles, were sepulchres and tomb-stones of twenty generations. Only patrician families could have tombs here. Here were the tombs of the Scipios, Furii, Manili, Sestili.

The first part of the Appian Way is called Via Porta San Sebastiano. At the beginning, the famous **Baths of Caracalla** or Antonine Baths, begun by Septimius Severus in 206 and inaugurated in 217 by Caracalla, although finished by his successors Heliogabal and Alexander Severus. Sixteeen hundred persons could bathe here at the same time. So vast were the baths that to the eyes of Ammianus Marcellinus they seemed like provinces. There were rooms for cold, hot and warm baths, splendid ceilings, porticoes, pillared halls, gymnasiums, where the rarest marbles, the most colossal columns, the finest statues were admired by the people; even the baths were of basalt, granite, alabaster.
Still today, the size and the majesty of the ruins of this great complex are impressive.

On the Via di Porta S. Sebastiano, close to the junction with the Via di Porta Latina and the Church of St. Cesario, is **Bessarions's Lodge,** called after the celebrated humanist, Cardinal Bessarion who was of Byzantine origin and contributed to spreading the cult of classical antiquity in Renaissance Rome.

Many years after its discovery, when most pieces of archeological value had unfortunately already been removed, the **Sepulchre of the Scipios**, a severe Roman monument, was enclosed within a large park between 1926 and 1929. The monument is more complicated than its name implies. A 4th century **Roman house** and **Christian catacombs** may also be visited within this archeological park, as well as the famous family's sepulchre. By opening up a well which is 40 feet deep, nine tenths of the sepulchre have been made visible.
Before passing the Porta Appia or Porta San Sebastiano, we see the so-called **Arch of Drusus.**

The **Porta San Sebastiano** (former Porta Appia) is in the Aurelian Wall, begun by Aurelius in 272, finished by Probus in 279. It is well preserved. At this point, the most famous part of the Appian Way begins. It is marked by landmarks of specific importance, such as the **Quo Vadis** Chapel, where, according to a holy legend, Peter had a vision of Christ.

Facing the Quo Vadis Chapel, stands the circular ruin of the **tomb of Priscilla** the beloved wife of Abscanzius, a freed slave and a favourite of Domitian, who died young. Statius (45-96), perhaps the best poet of the time, included in his «Sylvae», a short poem in her honour.
As well as vestiges of classical Rome, the Appian Way offers us the most suggestive evidence of early Christianity. Indeed, some of the most famous Roman Catacombs (as these ancient subterraean Christian cemeteries have been incor-

The OLD APPIAN HIGHWAY, often called «Queen of the Roads», is one of the most famous of all Roman roads. It was constructed by Appius Claudius in 312 B.C.

rectly known since the 19th century), extend in all directions beneath it. In fact, the areas destined by the Christians for burial places, used to be called «coemeteria» (resting place), while the term «catacomba» originally served to indicate the specific locality beneath the actual Basilica of St. Sebastian, where the land was characterized by a pronounced subsidence.

The Catacombs of St. Callixtus, St. Sebastian and Domitilla, are the most frequently visited and venerated. Guided tours are compulsory, so only a brief explanation is necessary.

The **Catacombs of St. Callixtus** show us the first Christian cemetery of the Christian Community in Rome, to administer which Pope Zephyrinus (199-217) chose the deacon Callixtus, who was later Pope from 217 to 222. The Salesians are now their custodians.

The **Catacombs of St. Sebastian** (over which since the 4th century is a magnificent **basilica** in honour of the Apostles Peter and Paul), received the precious relic of the martyr of the same name. The excavations begun in 1915 and continuing

84

*The Catacombs
of St. Sebastian.
The crypte of the Martyr.*

*The Catacombs
of St. Sebastian.
The three mausoleums.*

today, have brought to light a particularly important series of buildings, dedicated to the memory of the two Apostles up to the third century. It may justly be said that they form the most important monument of underground Christian Rome. The Franciscans are the custodians of these Catacombs.

The **Catacombs of Domitilla**, are called by the name of the Christian lady to whom this land belonged. She was a member of the imperial family of the Flavians. These are possibly the most extensive catacombs in Rome. In this area, stands the 4th century **Basilica of St. Nereo and St. Achilles**, which was discovered in 1874 and subsequently restored.

Between the Via Ardeatina and the Via delle Sette Chiese, at a short distance from the Catacombs of St. Sebastian, there is another place of martyrdom and sacrifice: the **Fosse Ardeatine** (Ardeatine Graves).
Just as the first Christians were innocent victims because of their heroic faith, so in this almost abandoned neighbourhood, at dawn on March 24, 1944, 335 Italians, mainly Jews, were the victims of the inhuman Nazi fury. Today, a grave and simple crypt preserves the same number of remains in sarcophagi, lined up in their death as in their martyrdom.

The **Temple of Romulus** was erected by Maxentius, his father, in the 4th century A.D. This Emperor also built the splendid Circus which bears his name. Unearthed in 1825, it is a magnificent complex: on the ample, harmonious rolling hills of the Roman countryside, as well as the ruins of the circus with its typical cylindrical towers, are those of a **villa,** also attributed to Maxentius (4th century A.D.).

The **Tomb of Cecilia Metella** stands solemnly on the brow of a hill on the Appian way. Cecilia was the wife of Crassus, a member, with Caesar and Pompey, of the First Triumvirate which ended the Roman Republic, paving the way for the Empire (1st century B.C.). On her tomb, which was turned into a fortress in the middle ages, the original commemorative slab still remains. From here to the IVth mile, the Appian Way remains as it has been since it was re-designed in the mid-19th century as a romantic road, littered with ancient sepulchres which have mostly been reconstructed.

The whole road, according to the original urban plan of 1931 was intended, to be surrounded by a vast protected area, from St. Sebastian's Gate to the limits of the Municipality of Rome and beyond. This was to be the famous «Archeological Park of the Appian Way» which exists on maps more convincingly than in reality, and was supposed to link up with the «Archeological Park of the Imperial Forums» in the heart of Rome, according to a project which has yet to be implemented.

*The Catacombs
of St. Callixtus*

*The Catacombs
of Domitilla*

THE VATICAN CITY

The **Vatican** has been the residence of the popes since 1377, only six centuries. Before the pontifical court was transferred to Avignon, (1309-1377), the headquarters of the papacy were at the Lateran. From that time, it can be said that there has not been a pope who has failed to contribute to its grandeur and its dignity, to make this holy hill an increasingly worthy seat for the Supreme Head of the Catholic Church. An uninterrupted succession of 265 men have sat on Peter's throne, many of whom were martyrs and saints. For twenty centuries the history of the Vatican has been the history of the world. Tempest after tempest, generations and centuries have come with their threats and perils: but all these have passed and the Vatican still remains.

Since February 11, 1929, the Vatican has consisted of an independant State called **Vatican City,** by virtue of the Lateran Treaties which resolved the Roman Issue between the Italian State and the Church.

In the Roman era, the Vatican hill was the site of the Circus Neronianus where under Nero, St. Peter the Apostle was crucified. His body was buried nearby and more than two hundred and fifty years later Constantine built a magnificent basilica on this spot, destined to become one of the marvels of the world. During the seventy-three years that the Popes were in Avignon, the basilica was so neglected that it was almost impossibile to restore it. Nicholas V decided to reconstruct it giving the project to Rossellino. On the death of the Pope, the work was suspended. It was Julius II (1503-1513) who began the construction of the new basilica. To design it, he commissioned Bramante who was to play the main role in this ambitious architectural enterprise, which took 176 years of work to complete.

During all these years, various projects succeeded one another (Raphael, Sangallo, etc.), until Michelangelo, almost seventy years old, began to build the dome. After his death the work went on according to his plans, based on the Greek cross as had been intended by Bramante. However, in Paul V's time, Maderno finally adopted the design based on the shape of a Latin cross.

Let us now admire St. Peter's square, in front of the greatest church of Christianity: **ST. PETER'S IN THE VATICAN.**

The square is unique. It is dominated by the immense suggestive * **Dome,** by Michelangelo. It is a harmonious poem of immensity. The dome rises gigantic against the background of the sky and its silver-blue colour merges with the same tint of the heavenly dome of which it seems the architectural synthesis. When Michelangelo's immortal genius conceived it, he must have perceived this sense of the absolute and infinite that would impress the soul of whoever saw it. And yet, the building of the dome proceeded among all sorts of problems and obstacles. Michelangelo was already advanced in years when he began to build it, after 1546, so that at his death (1564) only the drum of the dome had been completed. The rest of the work was completed between 1588 and 1589 by Giacomo Della Porta and Domenico Fontana.

The **colonnade** is the finest work of Bernini and

ST. PETER'S SQUARE is by far the largest in Rome. It is 340 metres in length and has a width of 240 metres. A beautiful Egyptian obelisk, 25 metres high, stands at its centre.

forms a superb entry to St. Peter's and the Vatican. The two large wings opening like half circles seem like the two outstretched arms of the temple receiving all mankind in one universale embrace. Nothing more harmonious can be imagined. If Bernini appears extravagant in some of his other works, in this colonnade he has shown all the power of his genius.

He was also responsible for the design of the numerous saints' statues which adorn it (140 to be precise) which were sculpted with the help of his pupils.

Bernini's brilliance in his design of the square is revealed in all its glory and functional impact during the benediction of the crowds, when the square is at its fullest on a radiant Easter day.

The erection of the **obelisk** roused great wonder and enthusiasm in the people. After conferring with many architects, Sixtus V decided to assign this work to Domenico Fontana. It was begun on the 3rd of April 1586 and the enormous monolith

was raised on September 10th, in the presence of a great crowd, with the aid of nine hundred men.

The **two fountains,** the one on the right, designed by Maderno in 1613, and the other on the left, in 1675 by Bernini, harmonize perfectly with the vast square.

In very large letters, right across the broad **façade** of the Basilica, the work of Maderno (1607-1617), are written the name and title of Paul V Borghese, who commissioned it. The **Loggia of the Benedictions**, above the central entrance, is used to proclaim the election of every new Pope and it is from here that he delivers his first blessing «Urbi et orbi» (to the city and the world).

Inside the **portico,** above the main entrance, is the famous **Navicella** (little ship), designed by Giotto during the first Jubilee year, and which has undergone a lot of restoration. Five doors open on to the portico, corresponding to the Basilica's five aisles.

The first door on the left is the **Door of Death** by Manzù, which shows the death of Jesus and that of the Madonna, the death of Pope John XXIII and death in space (1952-1964).

The **bronze door**, designed by Filarete, an imitation of that by Ghiberti at Florence, was also in the old basilica.

The **Porta Santa** (Holy Door) is opened only every twenty-five years. On these occasions on Christmas Eve, the Pope, following a special rite, goes in solemn procession to this door, and after a triple genuflection and three strokes of a hammer, the wall is removed and the Pope enters first. At the end of the Jubilee year the door is shut with special solemnities.

The modern reliefs which decorate it, are by Vico Consorti. Another two contemporary doors complete the portico, the **Door of Good and Evil** by Minguzzi and the **Door of the Sacraments**, by Crocetti.

And now let us enter the church, which is the impressive sanctuary of Christ built over the tomb of his first Vicar. The main altar, beneath Michelangelo's dome, stands over the **tomb of St. Peter**, definitively identified after the excavations carried out in the '50s and '60s, which will be mentioned in our description of the Sacred Grottoes. Before us, burning day and night, flicker ninety-five lamps.

In the **Confessional** is the statue of Pius VI kneeling, by Canova. Over the altar, the famous **canopy** of Bernini, upheld by four spiral columns, made with bronze taken from the Pantheon. But the glorification of the tomb of the humble fisherman of Galilee is the majestic **dome** rising up to the sky the multiple choirs of angels and blessed souls around the throne of the Most High in a glory of light, harmony and

Aerial view of VIA DELLA CONCILIAZIONE.

BERNINI'S FOUNTAIN in St. Peter's Square.

immensity.

In the niches of the colossal pillars are four statues: St. Andrew, by Duquesnoy; St. Veronica, by Mochi; St. Helena, by Bolgi; St. Longinus, by Bernini.

On the right of the pillar of St. Longinus, seated on a throne, is the celebrated **bronze statue of St. Peter.** Now let us start the tour of the basilica.

In the first chapel of the right aisle above the altar, we admire the ***Pietà,** one of the most beautiful works of young Michelangelo. The name of the young artist is chiseled on the sash that goes over the Madonna's shoulder. On the knees of the immortally young Virgin lies the body of Christ

who seems asleep. The Olympian severity of their beautiful figures is surrounded by a veil of sadness.

In the **Tribune**, four Doctors of the Church sustain the papal **chair of St. Peter's**, work of genius by Bernini.

St. Peter's Basilica is particularly attractive to tourists visiting Rome, on account of ist magnificence and grandeur for which it is famous all over the world. The figures are eloquent. The length of the interior of the Basilica, as revealed by a writing traced on the floor near the bronze gate, is 691 feet. (The outside length including the porch is 694 feet). There follow more

92

The majestic DOME OF ST. PETER'S, the work of Michelangelo, is 136 metres high and has a diameter of 52 metres.

THE MANZU' GATE.

The INTERIOR OF THE BASILICA OF ST. PETER leaves us openmouthed by virtue of its immense size. The central nave is 186 metres long and 46 metres high.

writings indicating the length of the largest churches in the world. The vault is 144 feet high. An arcade of the central nave is 75 feet (nearly equal to the obelisk of the square). The dome, inside, is 390 feet high; the lantern is over 55 feet high. Its diameter is 137 feet nearly equal to that of the Pantheon (142), which however, is less high. The perimeter of each of the four pillars supporting the dome, is 232 feet. The statues in the respective niches are over 16 feet tall. The pen of the Evangelist St. Mark, in the medaillon above the pillar of St. Helena, is 5 ft. high! The canopy is 95 ft., over 13 feet higher than the obelisk.

And if the Church is observed from above (for instance from the interior rail of the dome), one feels really giddy.

THE HOLY GROTTOES

The subsoil of the present Basilica, which corresponds approximately to the level of the original building dating from the period of Constantine is of particular interest. It is reached from inside the Basilica, to be precise, by a stairway within one of the great pillars which support the dome, which opens out into a semi-circular gallery known as the **New Grottoes**. In fact, this is the most ancient part, but it was opened later, hence its name.

Exacavations under the Confession have led to the basic discovery that Pope Paul VI announced on June 26, 1968: «The relics of Peter have been identified in a way which we may consider convincing».

Four oratories open on to the gallery, and several chapels, in one of which is the **Tomb of Pope Pius XII.** From this hall the vast space of the **Old Grottoes** is reached, which extend under the central nave of the upper Basilica, made by Antonio da Sangallo to act as a dampcourse to protect the flooring of the new building.

In the fascinating shadows of the three aisles with low vaulted ceilings, and the succession of two rhythmic rows of impressive pillar, the funeral monuments of about twenty popes, an emperor, a king, two queens, numerous cardinals and bishops follow, as well as precious works of art, all records of the old basilica.

THE WAY UP TO THE DOME

The entrance is inside the Basilica, in the left aisle, between the first and the second chapels.

The first part of the climb until one reaches the broad terrace which covers the central nave, can be made in a lift or on foot, up a spiral staircase. The view from the balustrade is facinating: the Bernini complex in the foreground, then a little further the shining meanders of the Tiber, and the city in the distance, make a very harmonious scene.

THE TOMB OF ST. PETER.

MICHELANGELO'S PIETÀ.

BASES · PILARVM
EX · LAPIDE · TIBVRTINO · MARMOREAE
IX · PONTIFICATVS · AN · XIII

Bernini's HOLY WATER STOUP in St. Peter's.

Turning towards the Dome, we are suddenly struck by the restrained tension of the sculpted ribs which run up it to the lantern.

Within, we face a gallery which runs round the drum, 53m. from the floor of the Basilica. The view from high up is impressive: Berni-ni's altar canopy, as tall as a palace, looks like a small-scale model from here. In the last part of the ascent, we squeeze between the two superimposed spherical vaults, which are more and more curved as we near the top. Having reached the top of the lantern, we can go out to admire the unforgettable **view of the city** from the circular panoramic balcony.

THE TREASURY

In the Basilica once again, going up the left aisle to the Monument to Pius VIII, under which is the entrance to the Sacresty, one reaches the Museum of Historical Art of St. Peter's, or the Treasury .

Right from the age of Constantine (4th century) the Basilica of St. Peter received outstanding donations many of which came through the Emperor himself. The generosity of the donators was such that in the following centuries, the Treasury was assiduously replenished in spite of the frequency with which it was disastrously plunde-red, especially on the occasion of the various Jubilees which have taken place since 1300.

Bernini's famous CANOPY covering the papal altar. It was commissioned by Pope Urban VIII.

The CHAIR OF ST. PETER in its masterful setting by Bernini.   *The inside of the Dome of St. Peter's (Michelangelo).*

THE LIBRARY

The «Vatican Library» was founded in 1475 by Pope Sixtus IV. It is impossible to calculate the value of this most precious collection.

In 1527, during the Sack of Rome, the Borgia appartment was seriously damaged by fierce soldiers of the Bourbons and it is to the credit of Leo XIII that he had it restored in 1889.

In 1973 Paul VI was responsible for creating a religously-oriented **Modern Art Gallery**, using fifty-five rooms starting with the Borgia appartments. It contains more than 800 works by the most important artists from the 19th century to the present day. In the sumptuous Sistine Hall are visible many rare manuscripts such as the **Codex of the Bible** of the 4th century, four copies of Virgil dating from the third to the fifth centuries, the Gospel of St. Matthew of the sixth century, the famous Palimpsest containing a large part of «De Republica» by Cicero.

Along the Gallery are ranged beautiful gifts given to Pius IX, Leo XIII and Pius X by sovereigns and Catholic Associations. At the end of the Library, in a room on the right, there is a precious collection of antique frescoes, among which the most important represents the **Aldobrandini Nuptials**, found in 1607. It is a pretty composition, part of a long frieze around a room, belonging to the first years of Augustus' reign.

RAPHAEL'S ROOMS

As soon as Raphael came to Rome, he was presented to the Pope Julius II by Bramante. Some rooms above the Borgia apartment had already been frescoed by Perugino, Sodoma and others, but Julius II decided to have them scraped and painted again by the young Raphael.

The *first room*, called the room of the **Fire in the Borgo**, was painted at the time of Leo X and it is the last room that Raphael saw finished. The principal fresco represents a fire in the Leonine City, miraculously extinguished by Leo IV, who made the sign of the cross from a window of the

The bronze STATUE OF ST. PETER. It is generally attributed to Arnolfo di Cambio is here seen in full adornment during a religious ceremony.

The VATICAN LIBRARY, foremost in Europe both on account of its age and its treasures of manuscripts and rare books.

Panoramic view from the dome of St. Peter's.

Vatican. In the background is seen the façade of the old church of St. Peter's not yet demolished. The group on the left is noteworthy for its vigorous and powerful design.

In the *second room* is the first work done by Raphael: the **Dispute of the Holy Sacrament,** finished in 1509. The subject of this magnificent fresco is the glory of the Eucharist, but could be more exactly called the glorification of Catholicism. The figure of Christ above, and the monstrance with the Host below, indicate His double presence, in heaven and on earth.

In the front of the Dispute is the so-called **School of Athens**. Its subject is Human Science, represented by an assembly of great philosophers of old times: a group arranged with great ability and including the entire philosophical school of Dante. Above the window **Mount Parnasus** can be admired, the mythical Greek mountain of the gods. Gathered round Apollo who is playing the viola, are the Muses and the most famous poets, including Dante and Petrarch. Raphael, although he was very young, already shows a mature technical ability in his arrangement of the figures on the two sides of the window, integrated within the outline of the mountain.

Over the other window are the **Three Cardinal Virtues.** To the left, the Emperor Justinian presents his code to Trebonian. This fresco was painted by Raphael's pupils. To the right, Gregory IX (a fine portrait of Julius II) gives the decrees to a lawyer. This fresco shows the influence of Melozzo da Forlì.

Heliodorus' room, the third, was painted in 1511-1514; it is so called from the fresco that represents the **Chastisement of Heliodorus**. Above the window is the scene of the **Miracle of Bolsena** (1264) when the real presence of Christ in the Eucharist was proved by a surprising miracle to a doubting priest: spots of blood appeared on the Corporal.

The **Liberation of St. Peter** from prison was painted in 1514. It was arranged around the window with great ability. The three different qualities of light, the moonlight, the splendour of the angel, and the torch-light of the soldiers, are finely portrayed. This fresco contains another political allusion: the liberation of the Church from its French and German enemies.

The **Meeting of Attila** is another allusion to the quarrel with France. The work, begun under Julius II, was finished after his death in 1513. Here we see his successor Leo X appear twice, once as Cardinal and then as Pope. The greater part of this fresco is the work of Raphael's pupils.

In the *last room* is represented the **legendary life of Constantine**. None of the figures were painted by Raphael because he had only finished the design at the time of his death.

The oath of the SWISS GUARDS in St. Anne's Courtyard.

Rooms of Raphael. The School of Athens.

THE RESTORED
SISTINE CHAPEL

ILLUSTRATIONS:

①

The **Sistine Chapel** was built by the architect Giovanni de Dolci for Sixtus IV in 1473. The frescoes that decorate it were begun in 1481. They were to represent the Life of Moses (Old Testament) on one side and the Life of Christ (New Testament) on the other, as was the custom in old churches.

The succession of these paintings on the two side walls is therefore parallel. Almost every fresco, in fact, is connected with the one opposite. As it is interesting to compare them, we prefer to proceed alternating from one wall to the other.

The first two frescoes, one on each side, were painted by Pinturicchio (1454-1513).

1. The **Circumcision**. An Angel with his sword stops Moses because he had neglected to circumcise his sons. Zipporah perfoms the ceremony. This group is especially fine and recalls the grace of Raphael; the heads, some of them portraits, are painted with the greatest ability. The panorama is enchanting.

2. The **Baptism of Christ**. God the Father is above between angels and cherubims; below is a dove, symbol of the Holy Ghost over the head of Christ. At the sides, John the Baptist to the left, the Redeemer to the right.

In the valley Roman monuments can be seen, clear evidence of the Renaissance character of this work.

The next two frescos were painted by Alessandro Filipepi (1444-1510), known as Botticelli, who took almost two years to complete them.

3. The **Story of Moses**. There are various episodes of his youth. In the centre, he draws water for the daughters of Jethro, having driven away the shepherds and killed the Egyptian; on the left, he guides the Israelites through the desert. These groups are painted with great ability, strength of dramatic action and expression in the principal figures.

4. **The Temptation of Christ**, which is the principal subject, is in the background. On top of a building, Satan tempts Jesus: «If you are the Son of God, throw yourself down». On the left, he asks Him to change stones to bread; to the right

he tempts Him, offering Him all the riches of the world, if He will bow before him and adore him. The fifth and sixth frescoes were painted by Cosimo Rosselli and Ghirlandaio respectively:

5. The **Crossing of the Red Sea**. Cosimo Rosselli was assisted by Piero di Cosimo in painting this fresco, made to commemorate the great victory of the Papal troops over the Neapolitans at Campomarte.

6. The **Calling of the Apostles** is by Ghirlandaio. We honour this artist as the teacher of Michelangelo. Here he has painted two frescoes, one of which is lost. Christ names Peter and Andrew His apostles. Few frescoes can be compared with this. Although weak in colour, this work shows great method and execution; the panorama is unrivalled. To the right we see the portraits of the Florentine colony in Rome, among whom is Vespucci, the Florentine Ambassador and Giovanni Tornabuoni.

Cosimo Rosselli painted the seventh and eighth frescoes.

7. **God gives Moses the Tablets of the Law,** but he breaks them when he sees the people of Israel in adoration before the golden calf.

8. In the **Sermon on the Mount**, we see only two scenes: the Sermon, and the Healing of the Leper. The ninth and tenth frescos were painted by Perugino, Raphael's teacher (1445-1523) and Botticelli, one of the initiators of Florentine pictorial Humanism (1445-1510).

9. The fresco representing the **Punishment of Korah, Dathan and Abiram** who rebelled against Moses, was suggested to Botticelli by a contemporary event: the rebellion of the Archbishop Andrew Zamomelic, who tried to call an antipapal Council at Basle. He was arrested and put in prison where he commited suicide. All the drama of the scene is captured by Botticelli.

10. **Christ giving the keys to St. Peter** was painted when Perugino was still young and it is certainly one of his best works. In the back-

②

ground we see two triumphal arches and in the centre an octagonal building.

11. Signorelli, who surpassed all his contemporaries in the art of painting the anatomy and movement of the nude, worked with Bartolomeo della Gatta on the **Testament and Death of Moses.**

12. The **Last Supper** was painted by Rosselli in 1482.

The two frescoes on the walls opposite the altar, belong to the same series. However, they were repainted a century later by Arrigo Fiammingo and Matteo de Lecce.
In 1508 Julius II, always ready to undertake new enterprises, ordered young Michelangelo to paint the ***Ceiling of the Sistine Chapel.** The gigantic task was begun in May 1508 and finished on November 2nd, 1512; twenty-three years later, he began the Last Judgement. The artist was not prepared to paint frescoes. As a youth he had been a pupil of Ghirlandaio's, but later had frequented the school of sculpture that Lorenzo de' Medici had opened in the courtyard of St. Mark's at Florence. Some painters were called from Florence to help him. Bramante had built the scaffolding but Michelangelo refused all help from Florentine painters and put up a new scaffolding. In the work of the ceiling, we have before us a revolutionary architect: the prophets, the sibyls, and all the other figures, are the creations of a titanic artist, who was able to singularly combine painting, sculpture, and architecture, exploiting his specific concept for the vault to dynamically integrate his powerful scenes. These follow the narrative of the Old Testament, Genesis in particular, in a sequence which proceeds from the exit to the high altar. The different pictures are:

1. God dividing Light from Darkness.

2. The Creation of the Sun and Moon.

3. God dividing the Earth from the Waters.

4. The Creation of Man, who lies on the ground. The Creator is about to touch him with his finger to give him life and a soul. This fresco alone would suffice to immortalize the artist.

5. The Creation of Eve.

6. The «Fall of Man». The tree of the knowledge of Good and Evil, with a serpent coiled round the head of the woman, divides the scene in two: on the left is the couple who are picking the forbidden fruit; while on the right, the two are being expelled from earthly paradise.

7. The Sacrifice of Noah.

8. The Deluge.

9. The Drunkenness of Noah.

The Prophets and the Sibyls in the triangular space are the biggest figures in this monumental painting. They are all seated and accompanied by angels or genii. They represent: 1. Jonah; 2. The Lybian Sibyl; 3. Daniel; 4. The Cumaean Sibyl; 5. Isaiah; 6. The Delphic Sibyl; 7. Zacharias; 8. Joel; 9. The Erythrean Sibyl; 10. Ezekiel; 11. The Persian Sibyl; 12. Jeremiah.
Careful restoration during the 80's has revealed unexpectedly brilliant colours which have naturally changed the traditional view of the colours of this masterpiece.
23 years passed after Michelangelo had decorated the ceiling, during which the Christian world had been torn apart by the Lutheran Reformation and Rome had suffered the worst sack in its history, before he painted the **LAST JUDGEMENT** on the wall above the main altar. It is unique, inimitable, stupendous and it conquers and dominates us with the splendid audacity of its creator who infused into it all his own strength. Above, turning to the left, is Christ, the implacable Judge, with his right hand raised in condemnation. The words: «Go ye accursed!» are not written but they are felt. The Madonna at his side appears placidly resigned to the hour of judgement. The others are prophets, apostles, martyrs. On the right of the Messiah are the elect: on the left, the sinners. In heaven, between the lunettes, are the angels with the instruments of His

AZOR
SADOCH

IACOB
IOSEPH

EZECHIAS
MANASSES
AMON

Passion. Below, on the left, the scene of the Resurrection of the dead: a group of angels, at the centre, bearing the book of judgment, blow the trumpets while from the open sepulchres the dead come forth to go to the Valley of Jehoshaphat. And while the good rise to Heaven, to the helpless rage of the demons, the evil ones are precipitated into the abyss where Charon with his boat and Minos, the infernal judge, await them. The Last Judgement, an epitome of the Divine Comedy and pictorial explosion of the «Dies irae», was begun by Michelangelo in 1535 and finished 1541; six years' work.

The face of the beautiful poetess, Vittoria Colonna, probably had its influence on the faces of the women in the Last Judgement. Michelangelo fell passionately in love with her. Paul III, accompanied by his master of cerimonies, Biagio da Cesena, used often to come to see the artist paint, and one day asked Mons. da Cesena his opinion on the work. «Your Holiness, these figures are fit for an inn, not for your chapel». Michelangelo's only answer was to paint in Biagio da Cesena as Minos. When the master of ceremonies asked to have his portrait removed, Paul III replied: «If Michelangelo had put you in Heaven, I might have been able to do something for you, but down below I have no power». Daniele da Volterra, known in history as «Braghettone» who used so much canvas to cover heroic nudes, had none for poor Minos.

From the earliest times, the Sistine Chapel has been the centre of sacred music. The great composer Pierluigi, known by the name of his native town, Palestrina, was one of the founders of chamber music in the 16th century and was in charge of the Papal Chapel.

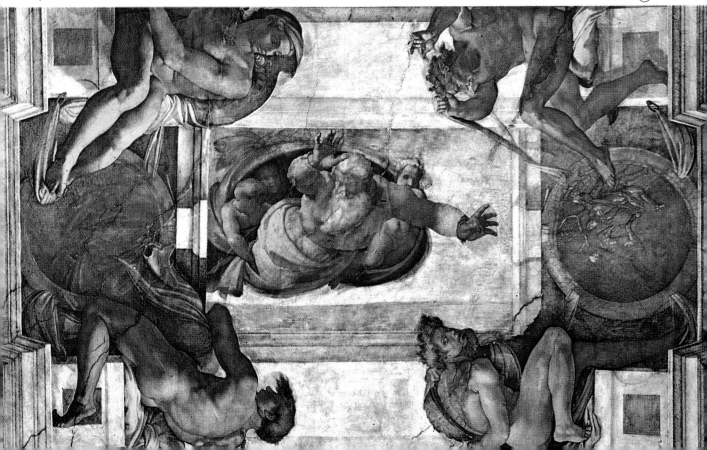

THE VATICAN PICTURE GALLERY

Pius XI was responsible for the present splendid rooms of the Vatican Picture Gallery. He commissioned the architect Luca Beltrami (1932) to build them. The collection, which was started in 1800 by Pius VI and enriched by his successors, was housed in various places in the Vatican Palaces before its present chronological arrangement. Passing through these rooms, we are therefore able to glean a rapid but significant impression of Italian painting.

Room I. Byzantine collection and various primitive painters.

Room II. Giotto and his school.
Here we can see the first steps of the Renaissance, beginning at Siena with Duccio and Simone Martini; at Florence with Cimabue and Giotto who lit the torch which first illuminated the sanctuary of our faith.

Room III. Fra Angelico.
The **Virgin and Angels**, a small attractive picture, was given to Pius IX by Lord Dudley in 1872. The grace of the «queen of flowers» is enchanting: against a background of golden roses the human flesh itself, seen throught the diaphanous garments, seems formed of rose petals.
The **Coronation of the Virgin** is a triptych painted by Filippo Lippi in 1460 for Carlo Marzuppini, seen kneeling at the left with his hands joined.

Room IV. Melozzo da Forlí.
Here are also beautiful fragments of a large fresco painted by Melozzo in 1472 in the Basilica of the Holy Apostles. The figures of the angel musicians are full of style and poetry, comparable to the noblest productions of Titian and Correggio, half a century later.

Room V. Bellini: Pietà.

Room VI. Crivelli.
The **Virgin and Child** is a beautiful picture by Crivelli who liked to be called a Venetian: «Opus Caroli Crivelli Veneti» — 1482. He was a great artist, unique in his own special manner and in richness of colour.

Room VII. Perugino and the Umbrian School.
The **Resurrection**, by Perugino, was painted in 1502. The fleeing soldier is the portrait of the artist, while the soldier asleep is Raphael's, who seems to have worked with his master; in parts of this picture, the hand of Raphael is visible.
The **Coronation of the Virgin** is Pinturicchio's largest painting. Many finely painted portraits are among the figures of the Saints. The Virgin is full of tender kindness and the group is skilfully composed.

Room VIII. Raphael.
His great work, the **Coronation of the Virgin**, was painted by him in 1503, at the age of nineteen, for Maddalena Oddi. It is one of his finest productions because of the exquisite grace of the angel musicians and the deep religious feeling.
Towards the end of the year 1504, he made a first visit to Florence and there he studied the methods of all the great artists. At the Carmine Chapel, he learned the dramatic expression of Masaccio; from Signorelli and Michelangelo the precision of line and anatomy; from Leonardo the fineness of modelling and the delicate beauty of expression; from Fra Bartolomeo — for whom he developed a life-long friendship — nobility of composition and skilful and dignified drapery. With surprising rapidity he rid himself of the defects of the Umbrian school. This clearly appaears in the **Theological Virtues**, painted in 1507 for the altar of the Deposition from the Cross in the Borghese Gallery. This belongs to the second period.
In September 1508 Raphael came to live in Rome. He freed himself from other teachers and schools to form his own. This is his third period.
In 1511, while working in his Rooms, he painted the **Madonna di Foligno**. Sigismond Conti commissioned this to fulfil a vow made to the Virgin for having protected him from a cannon ball that fell on his house, at Foligno, during the siege. It is one of his most beautiful composition, entirely the work of his own hand.
The ***Transfiguration**, one of the most famous

pictures, in the world, was painted for Cardinal Giulio de' Medici, who became Clement VII, for the Narbonne Cathedral. It was unfinished when Raphael died; at his funeral it was carried behind his coffin. Part of the lower group was finished by Giulio Romano; his hard colouring can easily be recognized by comparing it with his Coronation.

Room IX. Leonardo da Vinci.

The most famous exponent of the Renaissance studied numerous arts and sciences, as we all know. Here is one example of his mastery of the art of painting. **St. Girolamo**, (from the first Florentine period), is an extraordinarily powerful monochrome study of design and expression, which shows the artist's genius, although it is less popular than other works of his, such as the «Last Supper», in Milan.

Room X. Titian and other painters.

The gigantic stature of this painter cannot be ignored in any panorama of Italian Renaissance art where he played a major role. Together with Titian, other significant Venetian artists are represented here. Among the works exhibited, let us mention in particular the **Madonna of S. Nicolò dei Frari,** by Titian; **St. Helen** by Paolo Veronese; and **St. Bernard** by Sebastiano del Piombo.

Room XI. Barocci and Muziano.

The **Annunciation and the Rest during the Flight to Egypt** are by Barocci; **the Resurrection of Lazarus** is by Girolamo Muziano.

Room XII. Domenichino and Caravaggio.

The **Communion of St. Jerome** by Domenichino was painted for the Aracoeli Church in 1614, when the artist was thirty-three years old. It has no rival for simplicity and variety of the heads, for rich drapery, exactness of the design, expression of the passions. Here the figures are beautifully disposed. St. Jerome, the Christian Cicero, is receiving the last sacraments from Ephraim of Syria.

The old theologia, worn out with age, dying, is upheld by his disciples. St. Pauline, kneeling, kisses his hand, the faithful lion bows its head with grief.

The **Descent from the Cross**, one of the most forceful painting in this Gallery, is by Caravaggio, the freat forerunner of modern painting.

There are other fine works of Guido Reni, Baroccio, Sassoferrato, Maratta, Guercino.

Room XIII. Maratta.

Here are: the **Madonna and Child**, by **Maratta; the Martyrdom of St. Lawrence**, by Ribera.

Room XIV. Various subjects.

Room XV. Portraits.

There is a particularly noteworthy **Doge Marcello**, by Titian. Moreover, let us admire **Clement IX**, by C. Maratta, and **King George IV,** by Lawrence.

Room XVI. Modern Art (19th century).

Another modern building, completed in 1970 by the architects Tullio and Vincenzo Passarelli at the request of Pope John XXIII, houses the most interesting collections from the Lateran Museums. They are divided into three sections: the **Gregorian Profanae Museum**, with exhibits coming from archeological excavations made in the former Pontifical state, divided into two sections (I: Roman copies and imitations of Greek originals; II: Roman sculpture from the 1st century B.C. - 11 century A.D.); the **Pio Christian Museum,** founded by Pius IX in 1854 containing material which comes mostly from the catacombs and the ancient Christian basilicas; and the **Missionary-Ethnological Museum**, containing numerous objects of a sacred nature from all over the world.

The rest of Vatican City is a small, extraordinary universe that it is not possible to describe here, due to lack of space. We cannot however, leave out what is perhaps the most important architectural contribution of the 20th century to this exceptional complex: the great **Pontifical Audience Hall** designed by Pier Luigi Nervi (1971), which is entered through the «Arco delle Campane», for the Pope's weekly audiences and other important events.

Raphael. The Transfiguration.

VILLA D'ESTE

The idea and the erection of the Villa d'Este are due to Cardinal Ippolito d'Este of Ferrara, son of the famous Lucretia Borgia and Alfonso d'Este.
Ippolito d'Este was born in 1509 and his brilliant ecclesiastic and diplomatic career culminated in his being appointed Cardinal and, later, the Protector of France at the Court of Francis I.
At the Conclave of Julius III he was appointed Governor of Tivoli, and he accepted this post although the independent and rebellious nature of the people of Tivoli made it far from desirable in the hope of being able to use it as a spring-board for his future advancement. Another important reason which induced Ippolito II to accept this position was the presence of ruins of numerous Roman villas, the foremost of all being the one of the Emperor Hadrian, then the ones of Mecenate, Quintilius Varo, etc., which allowed him very interesting discoveries.
He took over his new office on September 9th

Villa d'Este - OVATO'S FOUNTAIN.

Villa d'Este - THE HUNDRED FOUNTAINS.

1550, received by the usual outburst of popular enthusiasm and by the usual deputation of leading citizens.

Accustomed as he was to the pomp and luxury of rich courts, he could not resign himself to living in the already existing Governor's residence adapted from an austere monastery; in any case it did not suit his plans.

He thus conceived the idea of building a villa in the country, which would serve as a counterpart to the grandiose palace he was building at Monte Giordano in Rome. The latter was to be used for receptions meant to foster valuable city friendships, while the former was to provide a pleasant rustic retreat suitable for longer and more carefully meditated conversations in perfect privacy.

Ippolito, in accordance with the best diplomatic traditions, thought slowly but decided rapidly, and thus the Villa d'Este came into being.

HADRIAN'S VILLA

Aelius Hadrian was the second Spaniard, after Trajan, to be Emperor of Rome. He was an intelligent administrator, restless traveller, a man without prejudices and full of imagination, an architect, a versatile genius and lover and protector of the arts. He was a mixture of the shrewdness, nomadism and sensuality of his country, and a real son of his times, the instability, tension and restlessness of which his personality reflected perfectly. He left us a clear, vivid, and indestructible picture of his soul in his famous Villa.

Hadrian's Villa is the creation of a man who strove after new things and old memories at the same time, a man imbued with egoism and curiosity. It is the fruit his experiences, nostalgia, desires and quest for the impossible. Some historians positively assert that Hadrian himself prepared the plans for his Villa and for the individual buildings

Hadrian's Villa - THE CANOPUS.

which it contains, and even supervised the execution of the works. Without subscribing to such an emphatic assertion, we must, however, acknowledge the fact that the stamp of the Emperor is visible in many buildings and that his will is omnipresent in the Villa.

To experience new delights or to relive the ones he had already enjoyed, Hadrian collected in his Villa all the most beautiful and the strangest things that he had seen in the course of his countless travels. We find here sumptuous Egyptian architecture, sublime Greek works of art, sun drenched colourful Spanish buildings, heating invented by the Nordic peoples assailed by the cold, licentious comforts of the Aegean Islands, and the latest Oriental effeminacy. Thus, the art, luxury, refinement, and variety of every country in the world sprang up amidst the solemn and peaceful Roman plain conjured up by the magic of the Emperor's multiform will.

The building of the Villa was initiated in 118 A.D. and continued uninterruptedly for twenty years until the death of the Emperor in 138 A.D.

Hadrian's Villa - THE MARITIME THEATRE.

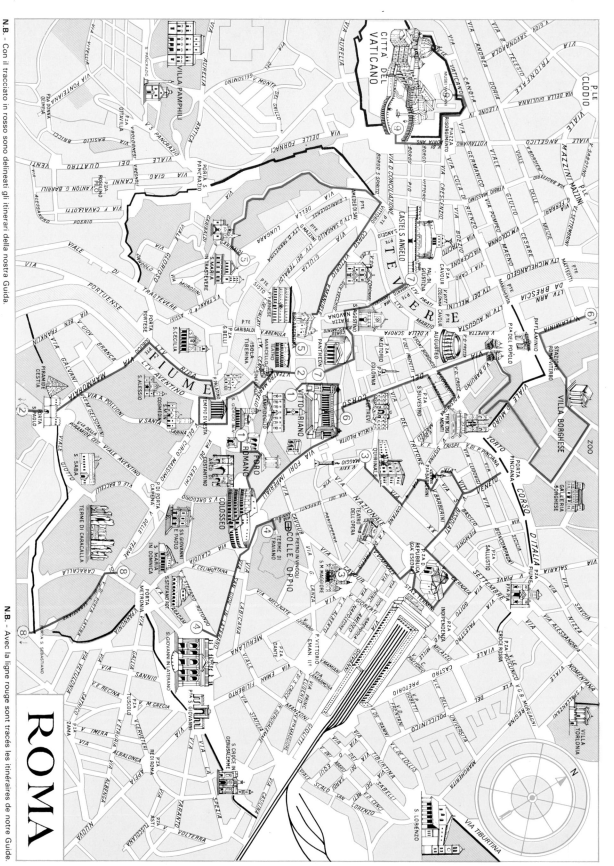

ROMA